What If
He Dies?

by

B. Renée Barnes

PUBLISHING

Little Rock

2019

ISBN 13: 978-1-949934-26-7

Published by Faith 2 Fe Publishing, Little Rock, AR 72205

www.publishyourfaith.com

Contents

Dedication   v

Acknowledgments   vii

Forewords   ix

1. And So It Begins   1

2. My Business Mind Was Totally Intact   11

3. I Had to Maintain His Standards   17

4. Handle with Care   22

5. Starting a New Norm   30

6. Where It All Began   39

7. God Proved Faithful   44

8. Memories: The Good, The Bad, The Ugly   50

9. Our Lives Changed Forever   59

10. God, I Need You Now   68

11. Committed to Live   78

Appendix   84

Scriptures for Your Journey   118

About the Author   122

For More Information   125

Dedication

I dedicate this book to the most courageous, thoughtful, and kind husband and father to our daughter. His sacrifice, along with his faith in knowing that he was going to be with the Lord, is the reason for this book. Watching him ride out his journey has caused me to grow into a better version of myself. I will always love EMM CHARLES BARNES.

"See you in the morning."

To the product of this love, Heather Charnee Barnes, I just want to say, "I love you so much." I've watched you navigate through this most challenging journey in your own way. We're moving forward together. I am so very proud of you and your accomplishments. Your father wrote to you in a book, "JUST BE GREAT." And you're doing your thang!!! And always remember our secret code, "Be Loved."

Acknowledgments

There are so many I'd like to thank for helping me get this book off the ground. Many thanks to Pastor Dean, for reminding me to write it just the way I communicate, which was so freeing for me. Thank you, Brother Clement Snipe and Prophet Jaiman McCamery, for being obedient to God and reminding me through a prophetic word that this book must be done.

To my wonderful parents who always believe in me, reminding me that whatever I put my hands to do, I can do, and it would be no different with this venture.

I have the best three sisters. My youngest sister, Tiana, was the pain in my butt, always asking what's going on with the book? Like a little gnat, just annoying. (laughing) I'm glad, though. My eldest sister Denise opened her home to me, where I wrote 50% of the book. Her organized and quiet home created an atmosphere of clear thoughts and some good writing. She would always set me up with coffee too!

To my sister Annette, I owe so much. Not only does she manage my singing career, but every idea I have ever had, she gets the ball rolling. All the leg work, she does it all. She can bring all my scattered and creative ideas into order.

To Michelle Steele, many, many thanks. You have brought all this together into something we call A BOOK.

And saving the best for last, where would I be if it had not been the Lord who was on my side? I'm grateful to God for His presence in my life and His patience with me on such a difficult and painful journey. To Him be all the glory.

Forewords

Understand? Understand what? I didn't understand then and still don't understand now. What do you mean he's gone? He is as big as life itself, a husband, a father, a thinker, a doer, a man's man, and so much more. So, how can, how do we, she, they, be expected to go on in life without the one who served as an anchor during life's most tumultuous times?

It was September 5, 2012, when my phone rang at or about 5:30 a.m. When the phone rings during those hours, it is either exceptional or devastating news. Either way, you quickly, yet hesitantly, answer the phone. The voice of my sister, Annette, on the other end of the phone said, "Emm is gone!" I instantaneously lost all strength in my legs and fell to my knees. "What?" I said. She repeated it, "He's gone!" At that very moment, it felt as if each word was a high-velocity bullet piercing through my heart. It was not that I could not hear my sister, but rather that my heart and mind did not want to process the implications of her words.

When I finally spoke with Renee, she said, "My baby is gone." From that day until this, I can distinctly remember a definite difference in her voice as she spoke those words. To this day, I struggle to convey with any semblance of accuracy what I heard. Emptiness, abandonment, shock, quiet panic, confusion are just some of the descriptors that 'may' apply to what I heard in Renee's voice.

As the days passed, plans had to be made. Despite the emotional trauma, a now widow and her daughter, Heather Charnee Barnes, needed to eulogize their loved one. I watched as my sister endured one emotional roller coaster after another. For months, I would not mention anything my husband and I did, were doing, or thinking about doing. I saw Renee's pain as follows: It's sort of like someone attempting to rip off one of your limbs with their bare hands. As the pull becomes more forceful and uninterrupted, your flesh and joints begin to separate, and there's nothing you can do about it. Once the limb has been completely torn from your body, the profuse bleeding starts. This hemorrhaging fosters weakness, compromises the independence, and leaves indescribable and often incessant pain. Some days worse than others.

Throughout this book, you will hear and feel Renee's heart: the joy and the sorrow, the hope, and the hopelessness. Moreover, you will experience not only the new and more powerful direction her God-given gift has taken but also the 'Village' that was forged out of her personal pain and grief. Renee shares her story from a position of purity and simplicity. You will hear the voice of a woman who appreciates and identifies with people who are genuine, sympathetic, and loving. Renee just wants everybody to be happy. In our family, every so often, we call my sister, Grandma Jr. or Mother Hickson. First, she looks just like our father's mother, Ruth Hickson. Second, her mannerisms are reminiscent of grandma. Last and most important, she chases peace. This is the woman who is laying her heart bare in the next pages you will read.

What If He Dies? is a captivating account of the journey of my sister and niece. How many people do you know that can bleed out, but no one sees the blood; scream at the top of their lungs, yet no one hears their cries; war with the adversary of her mind yet, speak peace? And all of this culminates in a ministry that assists others who have and are suffering just like her.

I may be the eldest sister, but Renee is the strongest, by far.

Much love always,

Annquenetta D.D. Thompson

B. Renee is a true example of God's ability to work through individuals. Her story is a powerful testimony of His ability to teach us lessons, heal us, and create masterpieces out of the toughest phases in our lives. This book is written from her heart, as every passage truly makes you feel as though you are living it through her eyes. I do hope that this book touches and helps others as much as it has touched and helped me. My husband has some health issues that he's been dealing with and, after reading this book, I stopped taking anything in his life or my life for granted.

Renees's entire family has a special place in our hearts. I pray for her ministry to help other widows continue to grow and nurture themselves back to a state of self-confidence and reassurance that existed years prior. When you read this book, I pray that you develop a deeper connection with yourself and a deeper connection with God, walking through a tough but rewarding journey of healing and fulfillment. To God be all the glory.

—Rhonda Kovacs

1

And So It Begins

IT WAS 5:20 A.M. ON SEPTEMBER 5, 2012. I can't say that I was in a deep sleep, but I sure was having a quality sleep considering my present situation. I sat up on the side of the bed when my cell phone rang. Turning on the nightstand light, I said, "Hello."

The voice on the other end of the phone was soft, yet clear. She spoke words that my spirit was prepared to hear, but not my soul. "Hello, Mrs. Barnes, this is Doctor... (I can't remember her name). Your husband passed at 5:16 a.m. He went peacefully without any pain."

As I put my head in my free hand, I asked if he had said anything before he died. I needed to know if he had wanted me to know anything at all, about anything, I needed to know his last words. After all, I was supposed to be the last one with whom he would communicate. I am his wife. This was a 35-year run; I should have been there.

She said, "Yes." The doctor mentioned that he was asked if he was in any pain. He responded, "No." They asked if he wanted his wife to be called, and he said, "No, I don't want to wake or disturb her."

I told the doctor that was so like him, always considerate of me. She went on to say that when she went back to check on him, maybe thirty minutes later, he was gone. The doctor said, "I didn't expect him to go so fast."

I responded, "He had a strong will. Once he was done with something, he was done. Besides, he didn't want me to see him die." He knew I would've made it to the hospital in ten minutes, although it was a 25-minute ride from our house at that time of the morning. He always told me that I was a great driver and could've been a cab driver. My sense of direction was impressive to him. I must say that I agree with him.

I thanked the doctor for her call and began to walk across the floor in my room. I moved around the bed, pacing from the window to the bedroom door, I walked in circles. Then, I stood in one spot and rocked. I was literally all over the place.

All of this movement was done in a room that was our bedroom for precisely 13 years. A place where we were intimate, we argued, we made up, we laughed, I cried, he pondered, and we figured out life. That room held all "our stuff," but now it would just hold "my stuff."

I gathered myself enough to make that first call, and it was to Annette, my younger sister. She was working the night shift at the Marriott Marquis, and I knew that her shift was almost over.

When she answered the phone, I said, "Annette, my baby is gone. He died. He's gone." I can't remember all she said, but the disappointment of his passing was expressed with few words and more feelings coming through that phone line.

I didn't know until later that she fell to a heap on the floor after she hung up the phone. Annette was seven years old when she met Emm, and when he passed, she was 42 years old. Do you get my point? The love went deep.

Annette took the responsibility of calling all of our family, including my parents, our two other sisters, and whoever else. I called my pastor, Dean Brown, and Emm's sister, Robin, in Ohio. I also called Emm's Aunt Elzetta in New Jersey.

I couldn't call my mom-in-law, Hermine, because she died in June of 2006, four months before Emm was first diagnosed with cancer.

I couldn't call Emm's youngest brother, Carl, because he died five months before him, after going into a diabetic coma. He was only 40 years old. The day we got the call telling us of Carl's death, as Emm spoke to Lonnie, his stepfather, I cried uncontrollably. Emm's biological father died when Emm was nine years old. Lonnie had raised him since he was thirteen years old. They were close.

I cried for so many reasons. The first reason was I couldn't believe Carl had died when I had just seen him, exactly one week before. The second reason was that Emm had lost so much weight from his third battle with cancer, and he was in constant pain. Reason number three was that while watching this weight loss, seeing him suffer and become so weak, I had become completely drained physically, mentally, and emotionally from worry. Yes, I was worried. Still, I was fighting to maintain my faith that everything was going to be alright.

What really sealed the deal for my emotional breakdown is what Emm said as he hung up the phone. He said, "It is a shame that my father will have to bury two sons."

I begged him, "Please don't say that." But, inside my soul, I believed him.

So, I called Aunt Elzetta, and we agreed that she would go to Brooklyn and tell Lonnie, my father in law. Telling Lonnie Sr. this news by phone wasn't even a consideration. Honestly, I am glad I didn't have to tell him the news that his stepson passed. This ninety-something-year-old man was now living alone because his wife died in 2006, and his youngest son died five months before Emm. His stepdaughter, Robin, lived in Ohio, and his eldest son from his first marriage, Lonnie Jr., lived in Alabama. Thinking about it now still tears me up inside.

I had already decided that after going to the hospital to finalize everything regarding my husband, my three sisters and I would head out to Heather's college to tell her the sad news and bring her home. I would not convey this news through a phone call.

My baby sister, Tiana, who was born three years after I met Emm, traveled with me to the hospital. Thank God that my wonderful pastor and his wife, Pastor Debrah, came to pick us up, although I would have driven myself without hesitation. The ride to the hospital wasn't sad. It was just a ride to the hospital, no deepness, nobody was crying, no going down memory lane, it was just right.

As I walked closer to his room in the Intensive Care Unit, where I left him the night before, my stomach dropped more and more. We had watched preseason football, and upon leaving, I kissed him all over his face as I would typically do.

It was Labor Day weekend, and we loved football. He played football at Stuyvesant High School in NYC and also at Iona College, where we met. He taught me about football, using the x's and o's, and I fell so in love with this sport! I was so serious, and I'm still serious about football. Don't play! It's not a game, well, it is. But you know what I mean.

Just before I reached his room, several nurses and supporting staff came to me, crying and giving me hugs. They called this 56-year-old man, the gentle giant, and that he was! The nurses knew me as the tall, bubbly woman with the 'fro.

Pastor Debrah asked me if I wanted time alone with him before they took him to the morgue. I stood at the curtain near the foot of his bed and answered, "No." I believe that I told Pastor Debrah, or maybe I said it to myself, "He's not here, and that is a shell."

I stared at this 56-year-old man who had always looked so handsome and distinguished but now looked so different. The empty shell I saw at that moment was not him. He didn't look handsome. Instead, he looked lifeless.

I was so shocked. It had only been a few hours since Emm had died, but this man wasn't him. I was numb. I'm not going to say he looked like he was sleeping, because he didn't. He looked dead! His jaw had dropped. His beautiful, light, and even complexion was compromised. Instead, he was gray in appearance.

My sister, Annette, who had gotten there before me, said she had lifted his jaw the best that she could. She closed his eyelids a little more and adjusted the expression of his face. I asked what kind of expression he had when she arrived. She explained that it was an expression as if he was expecting something, yet peaceful.

That sounded good to me. I am kind of glad that she arrived before me. Though I think I could have handled it, there are times I think I wouldn't have been able to deal with it. My beautiful, healthy, vibrant, 225-pound, 6-foot-2 husband was replaced with a 150-pound corpse. How was this fair? So, no, I didn't want any alone time with a corpse. Thanks, but no thanks.

One thing that touched my heart was how Pastor Dean took some time with Emm's remains. It was something he needed to do. I understood and was touched by this because, in the last year of Emm's life, my pastor would come to our home, then go to the hospital, then to the nursing home, and lastly back at the hospital to minister to him as often as he could. I am forever grateful because we had only been at Christ Alive Christian Center a year before Emm's last year of such a harsh and painful suffering on this earth.

After all of the necessary arrangements were completed at the hospital, I went back home to meet my sisters for the second most challenging task of my life. I had to tell our daughter, Heather, that the love of her life, the first man she ever loved, the first man that took her on dates and bought her flowers, was gone. The male version of her was gone.

Their relationship was like none other. Emm and Heather communicated on such an intellectual level, and it always blew my mind! I enjoyed listening to their philosophical discussions. I enjoyed watching them color Easter eggs from the time she was three years old, right up until the last Easter he was alive. Heather was 18, and Emm had to sit in a chair that last time. As they colored the eggs,

B. Renée Barnes

they discussed, as usual, the process, as if it was a serious science project.

"God, do I really have to do this? Do I have to tell our daughter that her dad died? I mean, like, really? God, really?" As her mommy, I was used to fixing everything, but I couldn't fix this. I couldn't change a thing about this. "God?"

Thank God for sisters! I have the best three sisters. We could all be on the outs with each other, but if, or when, something went down, all bets are off. Our oldest sister Denise, who is also Heather's godmother, planned to meet us at Adelphi University, where Heather was in her junior year as an undergraduate. Denise lived maybe 15 minutes away from there.

Denise and Emm were so close. They would talk while waiting for me to get out of class back when we were all at Iona College. They definitely were brother and sister, and they talked on such an intense intellectual level until the end.

Tiana, my baby sister, drove us. I sat in the front passenger seat, and Annette sat in the back. Then, the unthinkable happened. Heather called us, as we were driving out there, and said, "Mommy, I got a text from … (I won't give her name because I don't want to hurt her or make her feel bad.) giving her condolences."

This was now my third, fourth, or fifth heart drop in just a few hours. I mouthed to Annette and Tiana what

8

Heather stated. I, who am never at a loss for words, was at a loss for words.

Heather asked, "Mommy is this true?" It took a few seconds for me to respond, but I confirmed the news that no child wants to hear.

Things became a little dicey at this point because we still had at least 30 minutes to go to get to her. She began to explain that she couldn't breathe as I tried to help, telling her to take deep breaths. I was so concerned because Heather was asthmatic, mostly during the high pollen season, but I knew that shock and stress could trigger an asthmatic attack. I told her to stay on the phone with me.

Annette called Denise from her phone, instructing her to get to Heather immediately. Then, Annette started to call 911. At one point, it became almost comical because, between Tiana and I, we were telling Annette, "Call..., Wait..., Don't call... Yes, call! No, hold on. No, wait."

We didn't end up calling 911 because Heather said she would be okay. Eventually, Denise arrived, and shortly after that, we reached her side. We, my sisters and I, encircled Heather and hugged. God, help us!

Heather gathered some clothes, and we left. The ride back home was uneventful and quiet. I can't recall anything specific about our conversation. Emm had a beautiful and unique relationship with all of my sisters. He always used to say, "Don't mess with the McDaniel sisters!"

2

My Business Mind Was Totally Intact

NOW, I HAD TO PREPARE for the service. I prayed, "Lord, give me strength." I couldn't believe what was happening. *Am I dreaming? Somebody wake me up, please.*

In the days to come, I watched my daughter, as well as myself, suffer anxiety and sudden outbursts of crying. She slept with me during this time. We both needed the closeness.

Needless to say, my appetite decreased, and I had already lost 15 pounds during the last three months of his life, from all the running I was doing. I traveled from my job in the Bronx, to our home in Yonkers, to the hospital in Manhattan. Put that on repeat for 90 days. It is a wonder that I didn't lose even more weight.

The support of our family and church family was such a help. As Heather and I were in the funeral home to prepare the arrangements for the service and burial, my father, my pastor, and my sister, Annette, were all there.

Before I tell you about that experience, let me mention that, even with this life-altering experience, my business mind was still totally intact.

The funeral home came highly recommended by Emm's aunt; her deceased husband had been a funeral director at Whigham's Funeral Home in New Jersey, where Whitney Houston's and Sarah Vaughn's remains were prepared. Pastor Dean and my cousin, Bishop Eric McDaniel, spoke highly of this funeral home as well. Granby's lived up to their reputation. They were professional, gracious, and caring, but I also kept in mind that it is still a business. When they asked about us purchasing a casket, I mentioned that we ordered it online. Yep, sure did!

I had already asked Heather if she wanted to pick out the casket. She picked a beautiful copper casket for $999 that easily sold for $3,000 if we would have used the middleman. Save that money for the living. The funeral home just required that a family member be there to inspect it when it arrived from the warehouse. Annette took on that task. I had taken on that task for my paternal grandmother when she had passed.

The funeral home also asked me if I wanted those cards with his face on one side and Scripture or a poem on the other side. I declined and saved $300.

Listen y'all. Everyone must do what is best for him or her in these circumstances. This journey is so personal. Do whatever is comforting and makes sense to you. Do what you have to do. I'm just saying, don't put yourself in a financial hole while you're preparing to put your loved one in a hole. We have to keep living.

My bills never stopped coming, due dates on the bills didn't change, and my groceries still had to be bought. I still needed gas to drive my car. I never stopped paying tithes and giving offerings. You get my point.

On the day of the funeral, I was blessed to have Stacy B. design, and Rob H. print the beautiful 8-x11 booklets of my husband's life. Pictures galore. So many people helped me get through this financially and emotionally. I've never been prideful, and I accepted the help. I am not pretentious, and I'm grateful for everyone that loves me.

The funeral home mentioned that they would call the insurance company for me, but I told them that it wasn't necessary because Heather and I were on our way there. My Allstate Insurance office was a half-mile from my home.

What I'm about to tell you is a testimony of God's goodness and how God prepared us for my husband's passing 12 years earlier. Because I listened to the voice of God, I didn't sink after his death. I was able to mourn without the worry of immediate financial challenges.

Back in the year 2000, a friend of mine became a widow at age 40. I believe we all think about our mortality for a few days after attending a funeral. Well, after this young man's funeral, I couldn't shake this feeling that seemed to torment me for the next few weeks. I mentioned to my husband that I couldn't rest. I felt we needed to take out a policy with a larger amount of life insurance on us.

My husband respected the God in me, and we, along with Heather, went to the Allstate office. My husband, the financial analyst by profession, handled his business. Keep in mind, we were healthy, I was 40 years old, and he was almost 44 years old. Although we had insurance, it was minimal.

We were invincible, so why would we need more insurance? Because God said so! When God makes no sense to our little minds, we must learn to be obedient. And we were.

Why was this insurance decision so important at that time? The very next year, the terrorists flew airplanes into the towers of the World Trade Center. My husband worked in the area and was showered in the fallout from the buildings on that tragic morning.

This otherwise healthy man is gone now because cancer overtook his body after September 11th. With the policy he took out, we both were required to take a physical that was done pre-9/11. He was a healthy, vibrant man.

I don't know if the cancer would have been detected right away after 9/11. But guess what? God knew, and we had to act on His directions. When the cancer was finally detected in 2006, he was already at stage four. Thank you, Jesus! I was obedient, and it saved Heather and me from having to worry about our future when Emm died. Praise God!

When Heather and I walked into the insurance office after 12 years, we asked to see Ivette L., the manager that served us in 2000. I was glad that she was still there. She remembered us, probably because we talked about the Lord, in addition to discussing our insurance policies.

When I told her what had happened, she expressed great concern for Heather and me. She then made this statement, "Please tell me you kept up with your insurance payments."

I said, "Of course, why?"

She explained, "A woman just left here in tears because she thought her deceased spouse was current on his insurance payments. But he had allowed it to lapse, and she was left with nothing."

I told her that was definitely not my story; I always had my payments automatically deducted. My heart went out to that woman, that widow. Grief is hard enough, but not having enough money to bury your husband, at the very least, can cause even more devastation.

3

I Had to Maintain His Standards

ONE OF THE HARDEST THINGS I had to do was pick out my husband's burial clothes. "God, really? Any other time, but not this time. Please, God. No!"

When we first were married, I loved to shop for him; I would buy all his ties and shirts. Left up to Emm, it was all about gray and black. That was it, outside of the white and light blue shirts (corporate America colors).

But that changed after I took on his name. We were a good team when it came to his wardrobe. He was so meticulous from head to toe, and he was such a superb dresser.

He would say, "Don't wait until it looks like you need a haircut to get one." So, he would go to the barber when, to me, it looked like he didn't need one. He would shine his shoes "old-school" style, and though he had his shirts laundered, he would still iron them again before putting the shirt on.

I had to maintain his standards for this would be my last time to pick out his clothes. As I stood in front of his closet, trying to decide what he should wear, I doubled over in tears. Heather rested on our bed, trying to soothe her own pain.

I settled on a black and white, plaid-print, Nautica suit that had become a little snug on him before his final bout with cancer, but for obvious reasons, it would now be just fine. I chose a nice, crisp, white shirt with a baby blue, silk tie to complete the attire. I went to the basement where he kept his shoes lined up neatly and chose his favorite pair of black shoes that still had somewhat of a shine.

I made my way to the funeral home with everything, including a picture of how he looked in his healthier days. As I left, the emptiness and guilt I felt were the same as I had felt when I left the hospital. It would be the same feeling I would encounter when I had to leave the cemetery. I felt as if I was abandoning him, but I had to remind myself that he was not there. His body was a shell.

It is truly one's "remains." During this process, I tried to remember that his physical body was not who he was. I even remember telling Heather, as she picked out his casket, to consider his physical body his coat and the casket a gift box. We're picking out a beautiful gift box for his coat. When God comes back, he'll retrieve his coat. Praise God, that coat will be of the best quality too! Hallelujah!

On the day of the service, Heather and I, along with a few family members, had a private viewing at the funeral home before moving his remains to the church. As I entered the funeral home, I had probably reached the one-hundredth time of experiencing that sinking, heart-dropping feeling.

I remember going in and standing in the back of the room, looking at him. The room wasn't very big, maybe four or five rows of pews. I was able to see the profile of his body very clearly from the back. My cousin Eric stayed close to me. I watched Heather as she walked closer to his body. She took slow, steady steps, very emotional, painful steps toward her father.

As I watched her move toward his remains, these were my thoughts: *Who is going to give her that fatherly hug when she graduates from undergraduate school? Who will help her decide which graduate school to attend, giving her another hug when she graduates with her Masters? Who will walk her down the aisle when she gets married? Her husband won't know her dad, receiving the scrutiny that most fathers give to any man that walks into their daughter's life. Her children won't know her dad. Jesus!!!*

I couldn't imagine how she was feeling. Me? I couldn't take a step. I told my cousin, Bishop Eric McDaniel, "I can't feel my toes, my fingers, or my lips." Someone later told me that I was in shock. I believe it.

As I walked closer, I first noticed that now he looked like he was sleeping. The funeral home had done such an amazing job. Since he now looked more like himself, it somehow made it harder. I wanted him to wake up. Emm, get up, and come home, I wished. He looked healthy and just as handsome as ever. The only thing different was that he didn't have a short-cropped haircut; it was slicked down due to the chemotherapy treatments, which had changed the texture of his hair.

Was this all really happening? Was I really a widow at 52 years old? Was my 19-year-old daughter now fatherless? This cannot be happening, but guess what, it was happening, LIVE and IN LIVING COLOR!

We left the funeral home, returning to the house to prepare for Emm's celebration. I didn't ask anyone to wear all black or even all white. I wanted a sea of color. I actually wore a black, flowing dress (go figure) with an underlying taupe layer and a black lace blouse. I accented the outfit with a red flower in my 'fro. This dress that I wore, I had purchased online eight months earlier. I had never worn it before, and every time I laid my eyes on it in the closet, I pictured myself wearing it for Emm's service. That very thought scared me, even though I still believed for his healing. It came to pass, both his homegoing and his eternal healing.

4

Handle with Care

THE WEATHER WAS JUST PERFECT for Emm's service, a sunny and warm September day. The irony of it all was the date of his service — September 11th.

As I mentioned previously, my husband died due to exposure and the side effects of working near ground zero after 9/11. In planning his service, I had not paid attention to the date we had chosen for the homegoing celebration. He passed away on Wednesday, September 5th. When they asked me when I wanted to hold the funeral, I responded, "Next Tuesday."

I wanted this process over as soon as possible. I only realized it was September 11th when my friend, Michele D., called and told me she was trying to get to the service, but the traffic was terrible. I asked why it would be so bad on a Tuesday since the Labor Day holiday was over. I didn't understand. She said, "Honey, because of 9/11." OMG!!!

The atmosphere at the wake was so sweet and beautiful. Heather, being a music major, selected a wonderful variety of music as a video of family pictures were displayed. The wake was from 5-7 p.m. and the service started promptly at 7 p.m.

At 6:50 p.m., my pastor asked me if I was ready to have everyone line up in the back for the processional. I asked him to give me a minute.

I went over to the family and asked, "Do y'all want to get up, go to the back and march in, just to sit where you are sitting right now?"

Unanimously, everyone replied, "No." I do admit that my question was a leading question, but I didn't consider it to be a sensible thing to do. My father-in-law was ninety-something, and some of the other relatives were a little older with some physical challenges. Why would I want to subject them to muster up the energy that had to be so sacrificing, especially in this situation?

Besides, I didn't want to look at the faces as we walked up the aisle. The faces would have pulled me in, and I just didn't want to take that chance of crying. I had made a decision not to cry, and I was sticking to it. It wasn't hard to stick to it because I smile by default! And I smile even harder when I am nervous. I got shouted at for smiling all the time in Air Force basic training by the drill sergeant. So, yes! I smile!

The service was absolutely beautiful. I will not get into who did what, for fear that I will forget someone. I do remember that it left me feeling wonderful because he was so loved.

The highlights for me were many. My present church's support was overwhelming. So many people attended, my veteran comrades came, so many from Emm's previous jobs attended. My coworkers and people from my two former churches were there.

I was so touched that about 20 of Heather's college friends and three of her professors came all the way from Long Island to the "Boogie-down Bronx" on a weeknight. For those who don't know New York, that's a good 45-minute ride.

They remembered Emm because he and I were at every one of Heather's recitals at Adelphi. (He obviously couldn't attend her last few before he passed.) The love was so thick in my church that it seemed to take on human form. The love caressed us to the point that we knew we were going to make it. The service was just beautiful; Emm would have been so pleased.

As everyone left the building, we had a basket for anyone who might want to give to STAND UP TO CANCER. All proceeds went to the organization in his name.

The next morning was the burial. (Oh God, here we go.) I was so happy for another sunny day. The limousine came to pick Heather and me up for a five-minute ride to the church. I reached to open the door to exit the limo as we arrived at the church, but Heather, acting like her dad, said, "No, let the driver open the door. We paid for that." Listen, that statement gave me life. I wanted to laugh, but I didn't. I might have smiled or given a little chuckle, knowing me. This was the beginning of her trying to be my boss. My baby girl is overprotective and anything that has to do with Mama Bear, she is watching and listening. Honey!

As we gathered in the sanctuary for further instruction regarding the committal and journey to the cemetery, I noticed a veteran that was a patient where I worked. I couldn't understand why he was here. We weren't close like that, and he didn't come often to the V.A. hospital, where I work as an ophthalmic technician.

He was standing near the coffin, so I greeted him and asked why he was here. He mentioned that he was the driver for the hearse. He, in turn, asked me how I knew the deceased. I explained that the deceased is my husband, and he should be careful driving my husband's body. He offered his condolences, and I walked away from him, praying. I was praying hard in my head, I mean, really praying hard in my head. My prayer was, "Lord, let him keep his focus on the road, and strengthen that one eye that he has." I had checked his vision in the clinic enough times to know. Then I thought, *Well, he can't kill my husband.* But the point was to HANDLE WITH CARE.

The burial was short and sweet. In hindsight, I realize I had totally lost my level-headedness while at the gravesite. When I think back to the burial, I get a little embarrassed at my actions. I remember after the final prayer, as everyone was walking back to their cars to leave, I had Annette taking pictures of me smiling near the coffin. One would have thought it was a happy, joyous, photoshoot.

Every time I think about it, I feel embarrassed. As a matter of fact, a few people later expressed their concern for me since I laughed more than I cried during the service. As I reminisce, it was an uplifting service. So, I am okay with how I handled myself at the ceremony, but at the cemetery, I think I lost my mind.

Two days after the burial, my sisters, my mom, Heather, and I traveled to Rhode Island. I think I went because Heather said she wanted to go. I am sure she didn't know what she wanted to do either. I didn't know if I wanted to go or not go. The numbness and emptiness were in full effect by this point. We went and stayed for one or two nights. (I think. I was in such a fog the whole time) But the love of family led Heather and me by the hand when we were emotionally disabled.

A Celebration of Life

Emm Charles Barnes

Sunrise
October 6, 1955
Sunset
September 5, 2012

5

Starting a New Norm

THE NEXT FEW WEEKS were an adjustment, to say the least. I was walking around numb. I felt so helpless, but I remember, at some point, having an interesting discussion with my daughter. I asked her, "What are we going to do? Are we going to live or die?"

She answered, "Live."

I replied, "Not merely exist, but we will live out our purpose."

We agreed to return to our lives, our routines, and responsibilities, after two weeks. I would go back to work; Heather would resume her college classes.

I was always the mother that led by example. We were both grieving. Both of us missed that one man but from the standpoint of two different relationships. It was grief, nonetheless.

I made a deal with her; I said, "If you go back to school, I will go back to work." That is what we did. Was it hard? You better believe it! I am sure many others might not have agreed with our decision.

I also knew undoubtedly that one could not avoid the grieving process—no matter what. That is not what we were trying to do. My train of thought was: If we could be distracted for eight hours of the day and also be around people that loved us, it would be more helpful than harmful.

I felt that if we stayed in the house, doing nothing except crying and thinking, we would end up in a deeper pit. That situation would be harder to recover from when it was time to resume our lives. The way we both felt, if we gave in to our feelings, we would be home for, at best, two years. Let's be real. Meanwhile, back at the ranch, life still goes on, no matter what.

I am a proactive person who takes a firm stance when anything negative tries to attack me. How long have I been this way? I don't know. But I have definitely taken this approach since my husband got sick.

Once I got Heather back to school in Long Island, which is about 30 miles from me, I had to deal with being

31

in a house by myself. Emm was gone, Heather went back to school, and I was determined to make it.

My two younger sisters offered to stay with me for a while. I flat out told them, "No." I explained, "At some point, you will have to go back to your lives, and I will have to get used to being in the house by myself." This was one example of me taking a firm stance regarding my new life.

Being back at work was very hard. But I made a deal with my daughter, and I intended to keep the deal. Heather wasn't playing; she called me at my job every day, at various times of the day.

I remember one specific time that she called my job, and I wasn't there. She proceeded to call my cell phone, asking where I was. I told her that I was filling out the paperwork for that "sorry, little, social security check" for $250 you get to bury your spouse. (Don't get me started on that subject.) Seriously though, I believe, as I stated before, Heather was in "overprotecting her mama" mode. And she still is!

We both experienced many rough patches. There were moments of breakdowns, sleepless nights, anxiety, and fear. If you can name it, we experienced it. But the one thing I never experienced was being angry with God. Why would I?

I really can't say that I was ever really angry. Frustration? Yes! Anger? No. I don't know if Heather dealt with anger. I never asked her. I remember once or twice traveling to her college when things got a little rough for her. I am sure there were many times that I just didn't know about, and of which, I still am not aware.

The nights were just awful, completely awful. Because we lived in a semi-attached home, I screamed in my pillow when I cried. I didn't want my neighbors to hear me. Sometimes I went to the basement to cry. This went on for quite some time. The pain was unbearable.

I received many calls from a multitude of people who were calling just to check up on me. The love was just what I needed, but I still had to deal with the long, lonely nights. I hated every time I came home, put my key in the door only to realize that there was nobody there. No one would be coming in after me. It was the worse feeling ever.

Everywhere I turned, I visualized him in the house. When I was in the kitchen, I imagined that I heard him turning the key and coming in the door around seven, giving me a kiss. If I were upstairs, I would imagine hearing his footsteps coming up the stairs.

It was autumn when he died, so I would visualize Emm clearing the leaves in the front and in the backyard. When winter came, as I looked out the window, I would imagine him shoveling the snow and cleaning off the car. When spring finally came and even in the summer, I pictured him mowing the lawn in the backyard and sweeping the front of the house.

But the reality was that it was me doing all of the seasonal responsibilities which Emm had once fulfilled. I did receive help from my wonderful neighbors during the winter with the snow. I remember the previous winters when Emm had shoveled our next-door neighbor's house after she became a widow. Now, a neighbor from across the street was doing mine.

I must be clear and explain this: Please notice that I said, "I visualized, I imagined, or I pictured" seeing my husband. I never sensed him in the house, I never heard something moving around, and I never could "smell his scent." I have heard people mention these things as they share their experiences after a loved one died. I am here to tell you that was never my experience. I held on to the few dreams I had of him. Heather has mentioned that she sensed his presence from time to time, but that was never my experience.

I am grateful for every dream that I had of him. I would pray to dream about him when I went to sleep. I had a few dreams about him, but there is one that stood out above the rest. The dream left me so overjoyed during my grief. Also, my coworker had a dream that touched me so profoundly I wrote a song about it.

In my dream, I walked into our bedroom. My husband was lying on his side, kind of propped up on the bed on top of the covers. He looked so healthy, back at his normal weight, and as handsome as ever.

He was so excited to tell me that he got a PROMOTION. I asked him what he would be doing in this promotion. He said that he would still be doing accounting. (He was actually a financial analyst/accountant before he died.)

I asked him for whom would he be working, and he replied that he would be working WITH THE SAINTS. I remember saying, "That is great!" Then, I walked into the bathroom and panicked because I was concerned about what he would wear. I would have to tell him that I gave all his clothes away (which I really had done in real life).

But, before I could tell him that in the dream, I jumped up out of bed, wide awake. I had come out of the dream, remembering him saying, "I GOT A PROMOTION, AND I'LL BE WORKING WITH THE SAINTS!!!"

Thinking about it now, as I type, I am totally overjoyed because I am still so moved by his response. The spiritual implication of those words, to this day, brings me joy. Emm did get a promotion! He received an elevation, an upgrade from this life, and he is with the saints. He is a part of the cloud of witnesses! Hallelujah! Thank you, Jesus!

The other dream was experienced by my coworker, Fatima J., and I remember every detail of what she shared with me. I arrived at work one particular day, and she said, "I had a dream about your husband."

Teasingly, I asked, "What are you doing dreaming about my husband?" Here is the dream, as Fatima described it: Fatima came to see me in concert at my job. (As a singer

35

and recording artist, I actually give a concert annually for the veterans.)

At the end of the concert, she gave Emm a hug. He said to her, "She's gonna be alright." He also told her, "I knew that God loved her, but I didn't know how much until now, seeing it through God's eyes (from His perspective)!"

Fatima and I were both crying as she shared the details of her dream with me. That dream affected me to the point that I wrote a song called "THROUGH YOUR EYES." Here are some of the lyrics:

I know that You love me. I know that You care.

I know that You feel for me,
and I know that You are there.

But do I really know the depths of Your love?

Do I really know the passion You have for me?

I really can't imagine THROUGH YOUR EYES
how You see me...

Through Your eyes, You see where I'm going.

Through Your eyes, You see possibilities.

I really can't imagine THROUGH YOUR EYES
how You see me....

***

The song was recorded and featured on my sophomore project called "Healed!", and I asked my daughter to sing it on the CD because the Lord instructed me to have her to

36

sing it. As my mother observed, with Heather singing the song, it was as if she was talking to her dad. I thought about that and saw how God used one song for a dual purpose. How awesome is that? I wrote it and was talking to God. Heather sang it but was talking to her dad. Wow!!!

From the moment of Emm's death, time waited for no one, not even for me. Minutes became hours. Hours became days. Days became weeks, and weeks became months.

One night, I thought of something that caused me to make a mad dash down to the basement. I recalled putting all of the beautiful cards in a drawer that Emm had sent me while I was away in the Air Force. I had placed them all together with a red ribbon tied around them.

For the next few days, I read every card and letter that he had sent to me over and over. I needed to read them. But it made me miss him more, which made me cry more, which made the pain much greater. I am here to tell you that it got worse before it got better. But it did get better.

During that time, I replayed our lives together. I went from the time I had met Emm in 1977, to the point where I was in 2012—a widow.

6

Where It All Began

IT WAS IN SEPTEMBER of 1977. I was standing at an area on Iona's campus that they called "The Circle." It was centrally located between the administrative building, the library, and some educational buildings. I saw him as he walked out of the library. He was the finest man I had ever seen, tall, light-complexioned, and built. I asked his fraternity brother, Michael, "Who is this fine specimen of a man?"

Michael said, "M."

I responded, "M? What kind of a name is that?"

Then, Michael explained that "M" was short for Emmrett.

Well, me and my fresh self said to Michael, "M stands for MMM, MMM good!!! (the tagline for the Campbell's soup commercial)."

As Emm walked towards us, I didn't wait for him to get close enough for a proper introduction. I (being my outgoing self) bellowed, "Hi, Emm!"

He kindly waved as he walked towards us. That day started our journey. He was a senior, and I was a freshman. This fresh freshman hooked that senior! Many of the girls on campus wanted to be with him, but here I came on campus, hooking him.

But trust me y'all, that wasn't his plan. He planned to date me, and once he graduated, to move on. He told me that. But then, he fell in love. Things changed.

Emm was the strong, silent type and quite intimidating, if you didn't know him. He was a man of few words unless you managed to pull him in with a stimulating conversation. We were so opposite, but it just worked. He said the least, I said the most, and we met in the middle.

He never really showed too much emotion; I showed enough emotions for both of us. To make a long story short, he was a classic introvert, and I am an extrovert. We were so good for each other. He could calm me down, and I could make him laugh all day.

He also knew how to tune me out when I kept talking about everything and nothing, and still look like he was listening. I always thanked him for that. I wanted him to know that I knew his mind was somewhere else, even though he was staring me in the face. It wasn't that serious to me. He never acted rudely or said, "Stop talking!" He knew I would eventually run out of gas.

In 1980, I decided I needed to get away from New York. Emm and I had been dating for three years, and it had nothing to do with him, but all to do with me. I wanted independence but couldn't afford my own apartment, although I lived near the college in a room.

I was tired of my life, and it was just that simple. Church, school, work, repeat! When I met Emm, he showed me all of New York, and I enjoyed every bit of it. But growing up in the church, where everything was so strict, I just needed to get away from it all. It wasn't about wanting to live a "wild and crazy" life. I just knew that there had to be more to life! As Tamela Mann sings, I was "all churched out."

One day, in the fall of 1980, as I walked down North Avenue in New Rochelle, on the same main street as the college, I walked into a recruiter's office and joined the military. I never planned to go into the service. I never talked about it, but here I was. I took the test and qualified for the Air Force.

I forgot that my uncle, Bishop Charles Harris, had been in for 30 years, and his son, Charles Jr, was in the Air Force Academy and an officer in the Air Force. This is how much I had never thought about joining. It seemed like a great idea at the time, so I joined.

I left the following May of 1981 for Texas. That was really a bold and uncharacteristic move for me at that point in my life. Thank God for a praying mother and a praying grandmother, Grandma Hickson, my dad's mother (who I am very much like).

I believed I shocked the entire family. I shocked myself! But the military "owned" me, so there was no turning back. First of all, no one ever thought "shy" Renee would join the military. I had people tell me that I wouldn't last because I was too timid.

Don't ever tell me I can't do a certain thing. I will never try to prove you wrong if it's something that would harm me, like smoking. (By the way, I've never tried that. Being told that it may cause lung cancer wasn't the deciding factor. It was enough just watching folks inhale, and then have smoke coming out through their nostrils. What the heck? That was a BIG NO for me.)

But, if I am met with a challenge that seems to be or is beneficial to me, don't tell me you think I can't do it. Don't tell me you think I am incapable of doing it. Honey, you have just given me the strength to try.

7

God Proved Faithful

ON MAY 27, 1981, I left for Lackland AFB in San Antonio, Texas. My mom was so gracious. She always had a quiet, peaceful spirit. Regardless of how she may have felt about my choice to leave, she only showed love.

My dad, on the other hand, was quite upset and finally talked to me around three months after I was gone. In hindsight, he was hurt. He didn't know any other way to show it.

I really didn't know how much my sisters and first cousins were affected by my departure until later. Tiana, the youngest sister, was five months old when I left, so she wasn't affected as much. I found out, years later, how Emm felt and what he went through. But he never showed me. He just supported me in my decision. At that time, I didn't care who was affected. I just had to go.

The Air Force served me well. I appreciated my family more and learned who God was in a deeper way. I had a couple of boyfriends, not all at one time. I wouldn't be good at that. The thought of trying to "wheel and deal" like that would be quite tiresome.

Emm and I took a break. I told him I needed that. He was so hurt because he loved me. His mom would always tell me that he was still in love with me. She and I were very close for the nine years before he and I got married. When I was ready to come back to him, he didn't make it easy. I knew I had to be patient and let him take his time.

God proved faithful, even during my military years. I never had to participate in cleaning the dormitory (or barracks) on Sundays while in basic training. Why? It was because I was singing for all the Protestant services.

How did I get that gig? Well, I used to start singing when our drill instructor would call cadence as we marched. The next thing I knew, I was the one calling cadence. I began calling cadence with gospel overtones. They knew when our flight was marching down the road on that base! From that point, the word got out, and I was asked to sing for the services while in basic training.

After six weeks at Lackland AFB, I went to Shephard AFB in Wichita Falls, Texas, for technical training. I was learning to be a scrub technician. I would assist the doctor

45

by handing him any and all instruments needed during general surgeries. Eventually, I was told I would work in the specialty of ophthalmology. AHF-TA-what?

I found out that it was the study and treatment of disorders and diseases of the eye. I would work in the clinic doing diagnostic tests and assisting in surgical eye cases. I thought I was going to pass out the first time I watched a film on various types of eye surgeries. I said to myself, *It goes with my life. Nothing is ever simple; my middle name should be "extra."*

I thank God for my Air Force training. My profession is a profession that I still enjoy, and it has come full circle. I was taught the skill by the military, and I have worked to serve our retired military veterans for over 15 years now.

While in Texas, I found a church to attend. It was something I had to do. The need to be in church was always in my heart. I found a church that was predominantly Caucasian, and that was my first experience with their worship. I loved it! I even got to sing a few solos at the church.

I remember meeting an older man at that church, who was also a truck driver. Since he was involved in songwriting, he would send me music from time to time. Once, he wrote to me, telling me that the calling on my life was to sing the gospel.

Throughout my four-year Air Force commitment, I sang. I represented Andrews Air Force Base in a few competitions while stationed there. I competed in a competition at Travis AFB in California, and during that stay, I went to the chapel service on the base. At the end of service, as I exited the chapel, the minister shook my hand. He told me, "I don't know you. But God has called you to sing the gospel."

The bottom line is that God had His hand on me even when He was not my priority in life. Even though I was slack in my faithfulness to God, I was constantly reminded of His faithfulness towards me.

After leaving technical school, I was stationed at Andrews AFB. That was a "God-thing" because it was my first choice for permanent duty. Everyone told me, not only do you not get your first choice, you will probably never get any of your choices. I called home and asked everyone to pray. The rest is history.

I loved being stationed there because I was able to get to New York at least two weekends per month. I had relatives in the Maryland area, and I was able to attend some great churches in the area.

I remember seeing Carlton Pearson a few times. At that time, he traveled with his Bible and tambourine. More importantly, I experienced a different way of worshipping. I was able to go to a Friday night service in a T-shirt and jeans with sneakers or sandals on my feet. I was able to come in on a Sunday, wearing a sleeveless dress or dress slacks.

Remember, this was the early 80's, and that was a "no-no" in the typical Pentecostal church. My point is this: The Spirit of the Lord rested mightily in these churches, just as much as He did in the churches I had been raised. That was a paramount lesson for me to learn!

I always felt that there was more to life than how I knew church to be. I am, however, grateful for my church roots and foundational teachings. In hindsight, I think that is one of the reasons I wanted to leave home, in addition to wanting to be grown.

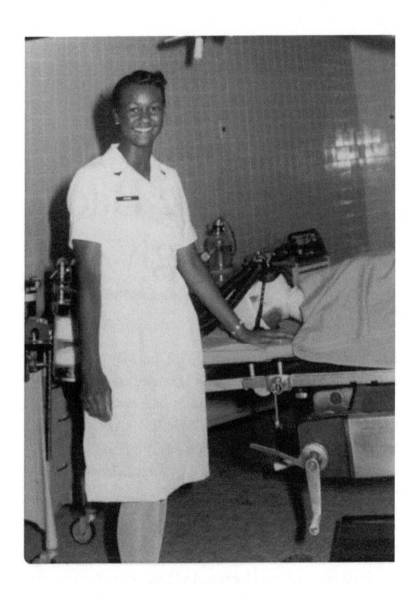

8

Memories: The Good, The Bad, The Ugly

MY TOUR OF DUTY WAS OVER on May 26, 1985. I stayed in the area, and Emm and I married on February 14, 1986. Yes, indeed! It was Valentine's Day! Emm had already transferred from the offices of IBM in Brooklyn, New York, to the IBM offices located in Manassas, Virginia. So, he was already living in the area.

Emm had proposed to me before I went into the Air Force. I returned the ring to him when I realized I wasn't ready. We went through ups and downs.

Emm was just good for me. And I was good for him. He was quite the stoic, analytical, confident, intelligent man that I needed. He was just so self-aware and possessed such a wealth of knowledge.

He helped bring me out of my shyness, which is nothing but fear. The confidence I should have had in myself, I didn't. I always felt that people were just more together than me.

He was more organized than I was. He helped me when I was scattered in my thoughts and with things that needed to be done in my life. When I panicked, he calmed me. He was so grounded, while I just kind of swung from one thing to another. I was good for him because I reminded him how to laugh a lot!

Also, I knew how to save money and pay bills on time. I guess the accountant wasn't interested in counting anything once he got home. That was okay with me because we had a system. He always said it was because of my budgeting and planning that we got our house.

He adored my craziness. Heather and I saw the laughter that others didn't see. I remember we used to sing the phrase from Nancy Sinatra's song, "…these boots are made for walking. And that's just what they'll do. One of these days, these boots are gonna walk all over you…" I smile now when I think of all those wonderful times.

I reminded Emm how Jesus was the way to go. He respected the God in me so much. If I never lead anyone else to Christ, I led my husband. And I'm so good with that.

We lived in Reston, Virginia, for a few years and then returned to New York in 1990. On May 1, 1992, we welcomed Heather into our world.

The only thing that was a surprise about Heather's entrance into the world was that I called her "Timothy" for nine months. No, I didn't find out the gender, that was part of the fun. So, when this 10 lb., 9 oz., Heather entered the world, I wasn't ready. I looked at my husband when she came out and asked, "Is it Timothy?"

He said, "No." Heather, the name I had for a girl since high school, made her grand entrance.

I thank God for her. He knew what was best for me, and Heather was best. Timothy never even formed. Can I tell you the only reason I didn't want a girl? It was because I was tired of doing hair. I fixed my sisters' hair, the hair of the girls in the neighborhood, 39 sisters in basic training, and so many others. At 32 years old, I was done. (So I thought.)

We were a little family that went through the trials and tests of family life like others, but we endured because at the core was love. We had made it through the nineties.

September 11, 2001, was the day that time stood still. It was the day that changed our way of living. It altered how we see the world and changed my life forever, though I didn't know it at the time.

I was working at St Joseph's Hospital in Queens, New York, at the time. As was the case with everyone else, I couldn't believe what was happening.

I was unable to reach Emm, who worked in the area of the World Trade Center. He was in Manhattan. I was in Queens, and Heather was in Yonkers. I was able to reach my family to have them pick up Heather from school with instructions to take her to my grandmother's house. I had no idea what time I'd get home. All the bridges were shut down, blocking the only route for me to get home.

The level of fear, anxiety, and anger that we suffered here in New York, and as a nation, was insurmountable. At around 3:30 p.m., I told my boss and coworkers I was going home. They reminded me that the bridges were closed.

Again at 4:30, I said, "I'm getting in my car and going home." I still had not been able to reach my husband; I didn't know how he was. He didn't work in the Towers but in the area. I had no idea if he was injured or not. I kept believing he was alive, and I just wanted to hear his voice, but that didn't happen.

At 4:30, I drove up Union Turnpike onto the Clearview Expressway that leads to the Throgs Neck Bridge. As I was riding on the Clearview Expressway, maybe four miles from the Bridge, the reporter on the radio stated, "The bridges are now open." I just wanted to get home to my daughter and my family. I honestly cannot remember if I ever heard from Emm by phone, but he evidently made it home.

He told me what he had witnessed. It was overwhelming even to hear. He stated that as he came out of the subway, all of the soot fell over him like a blanket.

He worked as an accountant at the Floating Hospital, which was actually located on a boat that was docked at the South Street Seaport. Until Emm arrived at his office, he did not realize how much soot had fallen on him. When he saw himself in a mirror, he realized it was a thick layer of ashes that covered him. It took a while to get it off his clothes and out of his hair.

After the attack, which happened early in the morning, everyone began packing to leave the area and get home by any means necessary. He and a security guard stayed because he wanted to get payroll done, and he was having difficulty doing it electronically with all that had happened.

As much as I knew that my husband always had a clear head in the midst of any challenge, he blew my mind with this one. He said regardless of what happened, people would need their paychecks by Friday, and he was determined to get it done. The security guard told Emm that he'd stay there with Emm as long as it takes. I believe they stayed until about 5 p.m.

Emm described the scene, explaining that many people ran toward the boat in an attempt to escape. But the boat was docked, it wasn't going anywhere. He told me that people were fainting, recounting some of the injuries he saw, and how it was just awful.

In the days, weeks, and months to come, many people went back to work and school in that area. But we had not recovered emotionally, financially, and physically as a city and a country.

Christine Whitman was head of the EPA. She stated that the air was fine. I never understood that statement. My father-in-law and I would discuss, from time to time, how this whole thing had affected or would affect Emm.

Emm reported to me every day that he could smell death in the air. I was so concerned, yet, so grateful for his life, not even knowing what we were about to face in the years to come.

B. Renée Barnes

9

Our Lives Changed Forever

THE BARNES HOUSEHOLD GOT BACK to normal life, and all was well. Emm worked at The Floating Hospital in Manhattan until he moved to another job in the Manhattan area. I remained at my employment in Queens until 2003.

There was one morning, towards the end of the summer of 2005, that I was getting ready for work. As usual, I turned the television on while I prepared Heather's and my lunch. The television was just about at its highest volume, which startled me, and I quickly lowered it.

I mentioned that to Emm, later that night, since he had been the last to watch the television the night before. He explained that he couldn't hear well in one ear. And Emm, being Emm, did whatever just to make do, never mentioning anything. I'm sure this is not unique to him; it's (more so than not) a man thing. I told him, "We do not self-diagnose in this house." So, I scheduled him for an appointment with the ENT (ear, nose, and throat) doctor.

The wonderful thing about Emm was, if I scheduled any doctor's appointment, he would go. Dr. Feghali mentioned that Emm had fluid on his ears. The doctor would drain them and insert tubes. He remarked that it was odd for a 50-year man to have this condition, but it would be taken care of. I believe it was in September when he had the procedure on the ear that was in worst condition.

Emm was happy with the results, and knowing Emm, he probably would not go back for the other ear. But "homey (I) don't play that." I was going to give him a short respite. Then, I was going to schedule the other ear to be done.

But in December of 2005, our world was turned upside down. On one Sunday, at my old church, my pastor at the time, Bishop Joseph Harris, called my husband out for prayer, just before the benediction. He asked to pray for Emm's mother, whom he had never met. On the way home, I told him to call her because something is happening if the pastor calls you out to pray for your mom.

We called her, and she said she had been in bed for a few weeks with what she thought was the flu. A couple of days later, since she had not improved, we took her by ambulance to the hospital. After many tests, she was diagnosed with uterine cancer which had already metastasized. My wonderful, beautiful mother-in-law passed that following June of 2006.

She and I were very close. Before Emm and I were married, I went with her to Ohio for vacation. Hermine could cook like nobody's business. She owned a restaurant long before I came into the family. I never told her, but I was so intimidated by her cooking that I never cooked for her. We would just go out to eat. Everything she made was just so incredible.

One day, during her final days, she called me on my job and said, "I believe the Lord is calling me home." I asked her was she ready, and she said, "Yes." That was the last conversation she and I ever had while she was still lucid before cancer went to her brain. Though the doctors gave her three months, we chose not to tell her that information, and she lived for seven months.

After her passing, we enjoyed our summer. Then, I scheduled Emm for a return visit to the ENT doctor to have the other ear drained. Dr. Feghali finished the procedure, and as Emm prepared to leave, he asked Emm to come back because he wanted to take a look at his nasal passages. That was a "God thing," for sure!

Well, he found a nasal polyp. He sent Emm for a CT scan to make sure it wasn't connected to a larger growth in his face. The scan showed that it wasn't, but the polyp still had to be excised and biopsied. This was all scheduled in September.

Everything was done, and on October 5, 2006, the day before Emm turned 51, our lives were forever changed. I thought that was the case when my mother-in-law died, but this was another level of "life never being the same."

Emm called me at work to tell me the results. He had a rare type of Non-Hodgkin's Lymphoma called Mantle Cell Lymphoma. He was already at stage four.

I couldn't believe what I was hearing. I maintained my composure, and we believed God together right then and there. I spoke with Dr. Feghali afterward, and he began to cry. He mentioned that he worked at Sloan Kettering Cancer Center early in his medical journey. Because of his medical experiences, he just was so sorry for what my husband was about to face. I told him not to cry. In other words, all would be well. I had no other choice but to believe.

What else was I supposed to do? Emm was a healthy man with no past medical history. Why was this happening? How are we going to tell Heather? I was scared, but I kept saying and believing, "He is not going to die."

Heather didn't have to know every detail of this journey; we gave her basic information that we thought a 14-year-old could handle. I distinctly remember the day we planned to tell her. Emm said to me, "So what are you going to say?"

I said, "Wait, hold up. What am I going to say?" And we both started laughing. We chose not to tell her that he had a rare type of cancer that was aggressive and considered to be stubborn. We chose not to tell her that we found a doctor in Manhattan that had only dealt with six cases.

We did, however, tell her that he had cancer and that he would be fine. We assured Heather that normalcy would continue, as best as possible, in the Barnes household. We asked if she had any questions, and I don't believe she did. She just said, "Okay."

I asked Heather about that conversation as I was preparing to write this book, asking her what kind of thoughts she experienced after that announcement. She said since we didn't seem worried, she didn't worry either. She saw our faith. She didn't see tears or any form of anxiety, so she believed as she saw her parents do.

At the point when we told Heather, I had already accepted the news. I was focused on getting things done. In other words, I was physically, mentally, and spiritually ready for the journey. It started with a made-up mind.

Even though Montefiore Medical Center made the initial diagnosis, I can't stress enough that a second, third, or sometimes fourth opinion is necessary. Additionally, the Holy Spirit and a great support system are of major importance.

The doctor at Montefiore presented their course of action, but I wasn't feeling it. What that doctor said to me did not make sense. How are you going to treat a cancer that is considered rare with a treatment that seemed very generic and non-specific to what we were dealing with?

We were provided the name of a doctor connected with Mt. Sinai Medical Center in Manhattan. As I stated before, Dr. Gruenstein was referred to us. He had dealt with only six cases, and five out of the six were still alive. The only reason the one passed is that he was otherwise unhealthy.

The doctor felt that Emm's prognosis was good because he was a very healthy 51-year-old. The doctor also mentioned if we had proceeded with the first doctor's suggested course of treatment, Emm would have never gone into remission.

At this point, allow me to mention that I prayed about everything throughout this process. I thanked God for His healing, but I also asked God to help us find a doctor who knew how to treat Emm's condition. I didn't want a doctor that was barely a graduate, but one that was at the top of his class.

I thank God for my niece, Clarissa T. She reminded me to get another opinion, something I knew, especially since I worked in the medical field. Nevertheless, I was so overwhelmed that I needed that reminder.

At times, things can happen when you are personally, directly involved with an illness. You may forget things or struggle with simple tasks or things that don't seem clear. Thankfully, God sends reminders from so many. I had to be willing to hear and follow the suggestions that were right for us, not the foolishness. I was no longer an outsider, but I was now an insider. It was up close and personal.

Emm had to go through aggressive treatment for an aggressive cancer. That made sense! Since there was no actual treatment designed for this cancer, the plan was to administer the treatment used for leukemia. He would receive eight cycles of treatment, with two spinal taps per treatment, and then we would see what happens.

I made a deal with him. I would make any and all appointments and pick up any and all medications from the pharmacy. All that he had to do was show up for each appointment.

His first treatment would have had him in the hospital on my 47th birthday and on Thanksgiving. But Emm wasn't having it. He rescheduled to Dec 1, because he didn't want to miss my birthday or Thanksgiving. I believe he didn't want to make it any more painful for any of us, especially Heather.

The night of November 30th, I was in bed next to my husband, talking to God. I said, "My life will really never be the same." I knew he would be healed. I knew he would go into remission. But I knew he'd always have to be checked to make sure nothing returned.

I cried quietly because I didn't want Emm to hear me, even though, when he went to sleep, he didn't hear anything. This is the man who, when pledging Omega Psi Phi, was placed in a closet with seven or so other guys. He found a corner in the closet, went to sleep, and snored. By the way, they were standing in that closet! My man was no joke; he said, "It's a mind thing." I still chose to cry silently.

The highs and lows of going through six cycles of treatment were more than he or I anticipated. I am grateful that Emm went into remission without having to go through all eight cycles of treatment.

If that had not worked, the next option would have been to have a stem cell transplant. His sister was ready to provide for that transplant. Watching his blood count, seeing him receive the transfusions, and having his taste buds change wasn't the worst part of the treatments. He never lost weight or vomited, and he continued to go to work in between his cycles of treatment.

The worst part was when he contracted shingles due to a compromised immune system. He said it was the worse pain, but he endured it. After all of that, cancer came back two more times as colon cancer. *Oh my God, my life, what is happening?*

While writing this part of the book, I am definitely taking more than a few breaks. I am reliving such a painful experience, especially since I have to write about him in the past tense.

10

God, I Need You Now

IT WASN'T LONG AFTER EMM DIED that I knew I couldn't stay in the house. For many reasons, Heather and I said, "It is time to move on." A few people tried to convince me not to move, and I understand they were thinking about what was best for me.

Owning property is a goal that everyone desires to achieve. But my health and wellbeing were most important. The suffering was too great. The only one I considered in making my decision was Heather. She didn't want to live there anymore for the same reasons I didn't.

First and foremost, we wanted to heal. That was not going to happen if we stayed there. Also, I knew Heather would eventually live her own life elsewhere, and I didn't want what comes with the upkeep of a house. I sold the house in 2014 and didn't regret my decision. We moved into a beautiful two-bedroom apartment building with new memories. We are still healing. God is good!

Someone asked me, "How do you know you're healing?" That was such a great question. I was surprised at the words that came out of my mouth and how quickly I was able to answer. It was the truth, and I spoke the words with no hesitation.

I said, "When Emm first died, I said, 'I'm not going to make it.' Next, I vacillated between 'I'm not going to make it' and 'How do I make it?' As time went on, it was only, 'God, how do I make it?' Before I knew it, I was saying, 'I think I can make it.'"

At the time I was asked the question, I was declaring, "I believe I can make it!" Will I ever say that I made it? Am I over him, as someone once asked me? I can say I will never grieve that way again. The choice to heal, along with time, has allowed me to smile more than I cry.

I responded to the question, "Am I over him?" with a definite "No, I will never be over him.' As I told one patient, I have learned to manage my pain. Some days, I feel no pain; some days, the pain is acute. I never know what will trigger the tears or the feeling of loss and sadness.

God, His Word, His people, and His music have been the best resources for healing that I could ever have. Let me not forget the importance of some basic, heart-to-heart prayer like "GOD, I NEED YOU NOW!" Throughout this entire journey, God has been, is, and will be my source. I never went to grief counseling, but I am a believer in counseling. God and the resources that we have in the natural realm point us to healing.

The place I am in today and the ministries that God has entrusted to me are only effective because of the road I have traveled. My mistakes, my carried-out plans, my trials, my tests, and my greatest life-changing experience, losing Emm, brings me to today. The chapters of my life from the time I was one year old until I was 52 had prepared me for the chapter that began when I turned 53. I turned 53 two months after becoming a widow.

About a year after Emm died, God showed me a vision so profound and amazing. As I looked through the kitchen window at our backyard, I saw Emm going in the ground, which symbolized a seed being sown. Next, I saw a tree with beautiful green leaves above the ground over his body (the seed). The leaves represented the souls that would come to Christ (reaping) because of my journey. So, I had no choice but to tell this story.

When Emm first died, I felt that the Lord was telling me to write a book. Of course, I waited for a few years because I was grieving. Evidently, I talked myself out of it though God gently reminded me every so often. I talked myself out of it because the thought of writing and reliving this pain was just not in my plans.

I decided that God hadn't told me anything; I began to think I had told myself. I rationalized that every person who loses someone they love wants to immortalize them in some way. So, maybe God didn't tell me anything.

Let me tell you this: "GOD knows and hears every one of our thoughts." Perhaps the Lord was listening to the shenanigans going on in my head and decided I needed to know, beyond a shadow of a doubt, that He ordained me to write this book.

About three years ago, I was sitting in church next to a brother who usually works upstairs in the children's church. Not only do I rarely see him, I really didn't know anything more about him except that he is a true worshipper. Those times when he is in the sanctuary for service, we sit next to each other. With the dancing, shouting, and praising that he enters into during service, it is like he is making up for the times he's not in the main sanctuary. As they say, "he goes in."

On one particular Sunday, during the offering, he turned to me and asked, "How's the book coming?"

I was shocked and asked him, "Who told you that?"

He answered, "Flesh and blood have not revealed this to me."

I began to cry for several reasons. One reason was that I was so shocked. Secondly, I hadn't even started the book. In addition, it wasn't me wanting to write a book, but it was God telling me to do so. Brother Clement touched my hand and told me that the Lord was not condemning me but encouraging me.

Guess what? I still didn't start the book. In the words of Fred Sanford talking to Lamont (from the sitcom, Sanford and Son), I can now say to myself, "You big dummy!"

God was so patient with me. I can't say that I didn't want to write a book. I just was being lazy, and I just didn't want to relive anything. But I knew I would never be "ready" to do it. Yet, it must be done. I kept myself totally distracted by trying to live my best life. I finally realized it! When I got tired of what I thought it would take to live my best life, I surrendered, and became focused.

The final straw (or encouragement from God) came through a prophet in March of 2018. Even though I had started to write a few months before, I had put it down. The word came that God was restoring to me the "wasted time." I knew exactly what that meant, and I haven't stopped writing since.

***

The last week of Emm's life was my biggest challenge. I kept pushing through. He was in ICU, and I made sure to get to that hospital every day because I was on a continuous mission.

Although I was always there whenever he was in the hospital, this time was different. He was on a respirator and couldn't talk back to me. During that time, I did the most important ministering I've ever had to do. It was greater than the biggest concerts and more important than singing in the prisons or before the four-star generals while in the Air Force. This time of ministry was more significant than any other venue. It was to sing for my husband.

I spent my days singing, reading the Bible, and praying in the Spirit around his bed. It is hard to describe where I was in spirit, soul, and body during those visits. It felt like each part of me craved something different. My spirit wanted to worship. I trusted God, and that trust was being renewed with every song, scripture, and prayer as I prayed in the Spirit.

My soul was trying to figure it all out and make sense of what was happening, while my body was so exhausted. All of this was happening at once, but I continued singing and praying through tears. If I close my eyes now, I can easily take myself there. But I really don't want to.

I remember it as if it was yesterday. I thought I was there on assignment just for him, but it was for me as well. God was building me up for what was to come.

The day before he went to sleep in the Lord, the doctor called me at my job with instructions to come to the hospital. She mentioned that Emm needed to go back on the respirator because his breathing wasn't good. She stated that he would probably need a tracheotomy. Emm said, "No" to all of it.

When I arrived at the hospital, she asked me to encourage him to please get the procedure done. I told her I would not. The doctor seemed puzzled at my response. I explained that I loved him too much to talk him out of a decision that he had made.

Then, she asked if she could talk to him in front of me. What she didn't know about Mr. Barnes was that when he made up his mind, that was it. I married him because of his strong presence, intelligence, analytical, and well-thought decisions, and he was the priest of our home.

As I followed her into my husband's room, I was so tickled because Emm had a way of looking at me with one brow raised as if to say, "Didn't I tell you my decision? We are not going to discuss it anymore." He was actually too weak for any of that, and his answer was still "No."

The doctor's final statement to him was that he probably wouldn't make it through the night. Emm showed no fear. I believe he was settled in his spirit before the doctor ever spoke those words. When she left, I said to him these words, "Whichever way it goes down, you still win. If God chooses to restore you with no artificial help, you win. If you choose to go to HIM, you still win because you're just stepping out of these overalls (Who says "overalls?"), your physical body, as you walk towards HIM."

As I spoke those words, I visualized it. I said to him, "It is a win-win situation; you can't lose!" He nodded his head, and we went back to watching preseason football.

That night, I didn't stay any longer than usual. Sometime around 9:30, I kissed him all over his face and said, "I'll see you in the morning."

He said, "Okay."

I believe we had two different meanings of "morning." I meant, "I'll see you Wednesday morning, right here on earth, in the flesh."

He meant the "1 Thessalonians 4:16 morning."

***

The title of this book, "WHAT IF HE DIES?" was given to me by God, which I thought was quite dramatic. As "extra" as I can be most of the time, I thought the title was a bit much. I have learned and am still learning that when God speaks, "Who am I to change His instructions?'

Obedience is doing exactly what the Lord says. As my pastor, Pastor Dean Brown, taught one Sunday, "Don't change the formula!" I had to contemplate the answer to this question, especially as I wrote the book.

At first, I thought it was a rhetorical question, even for me. I began to ask myself, "What is my answer?" Obviously, Emm died.

It was as if God was asking me, "What are you going to do?"

I mentioned earlier that I would keep living on purpose. I had to dig deeper to find what was God really asking of me. How many times do we deal with a challenge, a struggle, an issue, or a disappointment? How about the death of a child, a parent, a sibling, a friend, a love interest, or a death of a relationship? Everything boils down to choices.

I never asked myself, during his entire illness, "WHAT IF HE DIES?" I believed for his healing. Whenever the thought would come with the possibility of his death, I would quickly dismiss that thought. I believed that Emm would come through it, just like he had done with the two previous cancer battles.

Not only did I believe, Emm believed as well. I remember asking him, every morning of his last nine months of illness, if was he still believing. I wanted us to be on one accord, praying the same prayer. I read the Scriptures of healing; I made copies, putting them all over the house where he would be. I placed verses in the bedroom, on the arm of his recliner, in the bathroom, on the table, and kept extras copies. I even put a copy of them in the car and another for me to have at work.

I told myself, "Even if the breath leaves his body, I will pray, and life will be restored." It was just that simple. I never expressed that to anyone because everyone's faith isn't where yours may be. Yes, my faith had reached that altitude.

In hindsight, I realize that I was building up my husband spiritually, and my own spiritual strength at the same time. The last nine months of his life, before being hospitalized, I prayed and read scriptures for him in the morning, when I came home at lunchtime, and at night. Praying and reading the scriptures built us both up for two different outcomes. God was positioning my husband to go home to be with Him, and God was positioning me for a greater dimension in Him without my husband.

In looking back, I believe Emm had made up his mind to go be with the Lord before the doctor gave him his options. I realized that the journey we traveled was God, Emm, and me for a long time. There came the point where it was just Emm and God.

11

Committed to Live

SINCE SEPTEMBER 5, 2012, it's been God and me. The Renee that was alive and thriving with her husband is no more. I am now in a different place, a different headspace. I don't see life the same anymore. I had to unplan, undo, unthink, "un-be", un-plant who I had been for 26 years.

For example, I was no longer a wife. Every dream, goal, and plan we had talked about doing together died with him. The security and protection I felt with having him here were gone, and I felt so vulnerable. I actually feel exposed to the elements (i.e. the elements of being taken advantage of, of making bad decisions, of being harmed, of being destitute, etc.).

I've come to realize, since Emm's passing, that God has used it as a tool for me to empower others. How can I speak into others' lives, telling them what God will do on this journey if I don't believe it? God has shown me how to use my trial and catapult it into triumph. May the testimony of my altered life be the altar to change someone's life.

When one says "yes" to God, you really don't know what comes with that "yes." Being a Christian doesn't exempt you from what comes along with life—life happens. We must be prepared to go on, no matter what! And that "no matter what" came to me in so many different forms, challenging my faith more often than not. But still, "no matter what!!!"

When it was confirmed that I must write this book, I thought that was it. I knew that my ministry of song was impacted because the shy, fearful, insecure-at-times, singer was no more. Once you go through something that is so life-changing, certain things don't matter as much.

In trying to cope, I started writing a blog and had a Facebook page called The W.O.W.W. Factor. The acronym stood for Wisdom of a Wife/Widow. I would blog about the life we had together. I would share things based on my experience of being married for 26 years, explaining the challenges that accompany it. I had about 200 followers, and that was fine with me. It just felt good to write about my life and to release my feelings.

After a while, I stopped blogging. I really can't say why. Life goes on. What has never stopped is the compassion I feel for others who have suffered the loss of a spouse. It stops me in my tracks, and I say to myself, "Oh God, they really don't know what they're in for." And you really don't until you're in it. To this day, even if I don't know the person on Facebook, but I see that they suffered this same loss, I will comment on their page. (I used to send a message through the inbox until it occurred to me that if it was a male, he might think I'm man hunting. I was just sincerely giving my condolences.)

I was slowly working on the book. In the spring of 2018, I had a talk with God about how deeply sad I felt when someone lost their spouse. If I went to a funeral, my main focus was on the spouse sitting in the first seat in front of the casket. I rehearsed the emotions I felt when I was sitting in the same seat. I remember watching the John McCain funeral on television. Every time they showed Mrs. McCain, as she leaned her head on her son's shoulder, I cried for her.

I talked to the Lord about doing something with these feelings. I thought of starting a Facebook page, a private page just for widows and widowers. I asked God, "What should I name the page?" I thought of T.W.O. (Together We Overcome). It morphed its way into being called The TWO Village. I wanted a private page on Facebook for people to join, be safe, and say exactly how they feel. It was to be a judgment-free page where they can take off the mask and be free with their feelings.

This page is a blessing for me and for all who are a part of the page. I'm learning to hear from God more concerning this ministry. I became very excited and went forward with many ideas to help others with my same experience. I am reminded that everyone's experience is different though we share the same relational loss. After the loved one dies, people still have family challenges, personal challenges, work challenges, and plain old life challenges that they have to confront. This page is there for one to vent, read others' comments, encourage someone else, and share pictures of their loved one. It is a reminder that they are not alone. If someone is strong enough to give encouragement through a poem, a scripture, a Facebook Live video, a Youtube sermon, or a song, we are grateful. My motto for this precious group of people is, "No man left behind."

I recognize that the enemy will try to snatch our expectations, faith, and willingness to push through as we travel this journey. BUT God is still the greatest power. He has given us the power and authority to keep moving through tears at times. Still, we press.

I try to keep in mind that this life on earth is such a temporary and short part of the entire story. I am convinced that as fabulous as I was to my husband and as amazing as his love for Heather and me was, he would never come back to this imperfect world, full of imperfect people, even for me. I cannot blame him.

He made a choice to be with the Lord, and his assignment here on earth was completed. He wasn't a perfect husband but the best husband for me. He wasn't a perfect father but the best father for Heather. Many asked me if I would continue my husband's health ministry when he passed. My answer was no. God didn't give me that assignment, and God didn't speak to me, telling me to take it over. God had other plans for me.

I'm always reflecting on what have I accomplished since Emm passed. I must tell you sometimes I feel I've wasted so much time. Then, there are those times I feel like I am where I am, and that's okay. I'm okay. Feelings are just feelings, and the ones that make me better I keep. The ones that make me pity myself, I throw away. I may actually be just where God wants me to be.

So, finally, my brothers and sisters, WHAT IF HE DIES? I have chosen to LIVE. I believe there will be an explosion of ministry still to come in my future, of which I am still unaware. I'm glad I don't know it all yet. It would be too much for me to handle. I'm glad life is not a straight road. I need the winding roads, the left, and right turns, the stop signs, the yield signs, the red, yellow, and green lights. I will trust God as I travel, for He is at the helm.

Be encouraged family for we all have an assignment to fulfill "no matter what." Be blessed.

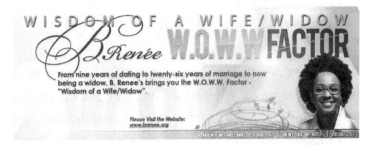

Appendix

THE WOWW FACTOR BLOG
WEDNESDAY, NOVEMBER 14, 2012

What does this acronym stand for? I'm glad you asked. Wisdom of a Wife/Widow. My goal is to share my journey of being a wife, and now a widow, what husbands/wives should have in place, and what we should be prepared for if we lose our spouse. This is also food for thought for those engaged or considering marriage at some point.

In most cases, the reality of life is that one will go before the other. Financial awareness and preparedness are vital. I want this blog to be a place where, not only do I share my journey, but you share your story and information that will empower us as individuals.

Well, let me begin. I am a couple of weeks from 53 years old, and I never thought I'd be placing an "x" in the box for "widow," as my marital status. I mean, you could not tell me that I wouldn't be married for at least 50 years, not 26! My husband, Emm, and I had so many plans. When our daughter, Heather, went to college in August of 2010, we became young lovers all over again, if you know what I mean (blushing).

We talked about Heather and education, Heather and dating, Heather and marriage, Heather, Heather, Heather. Now that she was in college, we were going to pick up from where we left off, Pre-Heather. Our first major trip was an Alaskan cruise together. It took some convincing on his part, but he finally got me to agree to go. I had a problem with being on the water for days and my feet not touching any land, but he always had a calming effect on me, and I felt safe with him around. So, I agreed. The one BIG thing that we didn't plan for was...CANCER returning, again! Oh Lord, not again! Not for the second time, but for the THIRD TIME! THIS TIME EVERYTHING CHANGED!

The WOWW Factor Blog
Wednesday, December
12, 2012

Bills, Bills, Bills ...
What A Joy

I hope everyone had a great Thanksgiving Day. Of course, mine was different, you know, the "first" Thanksgiving without Emm. My family was amazing, though. We were all together, and that meant a lot. Did I mention it was my birthday also? I was born on Thanksgiving Day, back in 1959. So that makes me 35 years old? Yes, that sounds about right! You figure it out. Either way, I'm FIERCE!!!

Today is not one of my brighter days; I feel a lot of pain at the moment. It's weird because I just don't know when it is going to hit. I can say this, though, it always passes. Thank God!

Well, let me just jump in where I left off last time. My dear, sweet husband was always so very giving. He took me everywhere, showered me with presents; he was just amazing in that way. BUT...yes there is a but! But, it was at the expense of not paying our household bills!

Now, me...I was the one that paid my bills before the DUE DATE. He was one that said, "I will pay them at some point." And he did; he'd make really big payments and catch up. (I think about it now, and it brings a smile to my face.) Then he'd start that same process again, paying at some point. (As I wrote at the end of my last blog, REALLY???) I thought I'd have a cow.

This was at the beginning of our marriage when he had his bills, and I had mine. You might want to know, "How then did I find out about his bills?" Easy enough, I opened ALL the mail. He had no problem with that; he was just "EASY" (singing), " EASY like Sunday morning."Anyway, I'd see late payment fees; I'd see cable and phone shut off notices. I saw those bills, and yes, I immediately went into labor, I was about to have that cow!

Did I mention that Emm was an accountant/ financial analyst? You gotta love him. Well, I did! He just didn't want to deal with numbers when he got home, so I called for a meeting. We had our meeting of the minds. We decided that we'd put all our bills TOGETHER and put our money TOGETHER. Everyone (meaning, he and I) came from the meeting very satisfied. He didn't have to deal with due dates and writing checks, and I didn't have to worry about anything being shut off.

Folks, recognize that one of the biggest areas that can break up a marriage is MONEY. What worked for us might not work for you, but make sure you discuss it and come to a decision that you both can live with.

Even though I was the one that physically wrote out the checks, Emm knew what was in the account, what bills were coming in, and what was being paid out. When there were challenges in the finances, without question, he'd figure it out. Is there ever a perfect plan? NO, but we started with A PLAN. I would always tell him how much I loved him for trusting me totally with the money, and I didn't let him down. (Ok, now I'm tearing up.) I also recognized that he was the head of the household, and me being in charge of the finances took nothing away from him as a man. I respected him highly.

One of my goals in doing this blog is to remind wives and husbands how important it is to know what is going on in your own household, FINANCIALLY. Remember, it should not be a " yours vs. mine" relationship. It should be an "our" relationship. You are building a life together. It is never too late to make a positive change in your relationship.

My father made a statement once that was so true. He said, "It's okay not to know, but it's not okay not to learn!" So, learn, build, and grow together!

I'm not an expert; I don't have degrees in marriage counseling. I am just a woman that has just decided to invite you into my world, my most precious memories, hoping that my experience can be of some help to you. My own experience, coupled with other folks' experiences, has brought me to that place of W.O.W.W.

I really pray that I'm helping someone along the way. God bless you, and be well.

THE WOWW FACTOR BLOG
DECEMBER 23, 2012
THE JOURNEY

Today is one of those difficult days, and I guess it should be expected since it has only been 2.5 months that Emm has gone to the "REAL WORLD." Someone used that term to say where he is, and I said, "That's it, exactly!" Also, I wanted to recommend a book that my pastor gave me when my husband first passed. It's by Tony Cooke, "LIFE AFTER DEATH." It's an easy read and an excellent source for healing, a book to minister to the loved one that is left here. When my pastor first gave it to me, I read a few pages, decided that I was fine, and I had this confidence of "I got this."

Well, in the last few weeks, the pain has intensified, and I realized despite how many people said, "you're strong," I felt like I was going to come crashing down at any point. It wasn't going to be pretty. Then, I remembered the book. I searched high and low in my house to find that book because I needed something in writing that just might relate to what I was feeling, and this book has not let me down.

Well, folks, let me start from the beginning of this journey. Feb 14, 1986, Emm and I spoke the words, "in sickness and in health, 'til death do us part." I was 26, and he was 30. Both of us were quite healthy and without a care in the world. Why should we think about sickness or dying? I mean we were invincible! This type of thinking isn't uncommon to healthy young folks.

Today I'd like to share some thoughts on basic healthcare. Young married couples, engaged couples, even single folk, have to be proactive in this area. I pray that married couples that have been married a while (let's say over seven years) should hopefully be advising and mentoring young couples in these areas. If not, then let me share it with you as well. It is better late than never.

It is very, very important to make sure that you get a YEARLY physical, without hesitation. Women, along with our physicals, we should get our YEARLY gynecological exams and mammography tests. Men, you must get all that is needed to keep you healthy as well. We must remember that as much as we "hate" going to the doctor, if something is going on in our body, it is not going away just because you don't want to go. We must be proactive with our health, and be an informed and compliant patient.

91

Ladies, statistics have shown that one of the reasons married men outlive single men is because of the wife encouraging him to go to the doctor. Ladies, encourage, nag, or (MARRIED LADIES ONLY) promise them goodies (wink, wink) whatever you have to do to convince them to go for their appointments. Remind them that staying healthy isn't just about them, but about you and the rest of the family.

I realized early in our marriage that Emm just didn't go to the doctor; it wasn't that he was afraid. He was the epitome of a healthy young man. He just didn't go. "Nothing hurts, no pain, so why bother?" Can anyone relate to that mentality? I mean, he didn't even know what insurance he had; I found that to be so funny. I snapped on him for days. I remember calling IBM Human Resources and getting his insurance information.

From the time I began making his yearly physical, he would go. If you see where you have to do the leg work for your spouse to go to the doctor, DO IT! Love your spouse to life, a HEALTHY LIFE! Husbands, you might be the one that has to help your wife along. JUST DO IT!

Life was great. We were doing well. Yes, we had our ups and downs, but we loved each other too much to let external things come between us. We wanted our marriage to work, so we fought hard together even in the seemingly roughest of times. He was so easygoing (his nickname in college was Easy), and I was drama. I was always concerned about life; he just "rolled with it." He was the listener; I just didn't know how to stop talking (mouth almighty). There are no two people alike, but in the words of Tim Gunn (Project Runway), "Make it work." And we did just that.

There was another major area in our marriage that I found out he was pretty nonchalant. Talking about living up to your nickname, EASY... there is an expression that is out now that I wished was out back then because I would have used it with all the passion I could have gathered up. That expression is, "REALLY?"

THE WOWW FACTOR BLOG
THURSDAY, JANUARY 31, 2013

WISINDOWED -
(WIS-IN-DOWED) ...

I started the year off pretty busy, and my pace has not lessened. I don't know if that's good or bad. I guess I'll see soon enough. Busy keeps me sane and keeps me from ending up in that dark place. I still choose to LIVE, LOVE, LAUGH, even through the tears.

You know, I always forget at the beginning of the year that I have to fill out my daughter's FAFSA (Free Application for Federal Student Aid) form. I just hate doing these forms, but it helps financially with a daughter in college. Filling out this form was not foreign at all because my husband and I would do it together every year. This is another example of knowing what was going on with the business of the house. Imagine if I didn't know about this application and simply ignored it due to everything I'm feeling these days.

Now that would be just tragic; who doesn't need financial assistance for a child in college? What was difficult about filling out this form was that it reminded me that I am WIDOWED! Man, how I hate that word and how it makes me feel. Then I had to check the box that stated her father was DECEASED, and I hate that word too!!! I'm not too comfortable with the word single either, probably because once you've been happily married and are widowed, single now is not the same has single before ever being married. You see life with a different set of eyes. With that said, I have declared myself WISINDOWED!

It's a combination of WI from wisdom, SIN from single, and DOWED from widowed. I FEEL BETTER ALREADY! Now, to figure out how to get that word on any and every demography needed for anything and everything, hmmm. When life serves you lemons, make lemon frosted pound cake. (You thought I was going to say lemonade. GOTCHA!) By the way, have you tasted Starbucks' lemon frosted pound cake? The way the cake ministers to me, nothing should taste that good!! That was random, but anyway...

If you remember in my last blog, I mentioned how sometimes things happen that you have no control over... LIFE HAPPENS. The question is: What do you do when life happens? Do you crawl into a corner, cry, and hope it goes away? Do you look at the situation in the face and handle it? My husband would always say, "I ain't going out like that!," meaning, "I am going to fight until the end." That is what he did, and that's what I will continue to do.

Life happened when we returned to New York after being in Virginia for many years. Emm had no job. Although IBM had confirmed a job, there was none. We honestly didn't know it would be so very hard for him to find a job. The biggest problem was "you're overqualified." What impressed me with my husband was that he never laid around, waiting for the "white collar" job to come around. This man went from handling U.S. Navy accounts with IBM to working in a supermarket (Grand Union) at night stocking shelves from 10 pm to 5 am. He took temp jobs in accounting until he found a permanent job, a year and a half later.

No one is exempt from life's challenges. What makes the difference is how you handle life. Always know life is a process, and we are forever maturing in how we deal with challenges. So don't beat yourself up if you don't get it right the first time. Listen to those that know, learn from the situations, and deal with it. Be PROACTIVE!

Love you guys, and don't forget I'm NOT single. I'm NOT widowed any longer. I AM WISINDOWED!!! HOLLA!!!!

THE WOWW FACTOR BLOG
MONDAY, MARCH 4 2013
...BUT WE DID IT TO-GETHER!!!

This thing called time is hard to figure out at times. Time doesn't wait or stop for anyone. Sometimes I feel like time is standing still, and at other times, time feels like it's getting away from me. Either way, I missed you guys, I hope you missed me too.

Since the last blog, there was a wonderful day set aside, called Valentine's Day. I hope everyone enjoyed and showed love to someone, even if only to yourself. You deserved it.

Well, guys, that day was the hardest day yet since Emm's been gone. I mean really, really the hardest day of my life. Put it this way. If I could bottle up the pain, the bottle would explode just from the intensity alone. Valentine's Day was also our 27th anniversary, need I say more? But let me tell you how I got through it, I always have a plan these days, I have made a determination that I am not going down. My daughter, Heather and I, met in the city (New York) to see The Phantom of the Opera.

When I saw her face, that beautiful face immediately made me feel better. She hugged me, gave me a card and a gift. The play, in one word, was PHENOMENAL! It was simply AMAZING. By the way, it is their 25th anniversary on Broadway, so the tickets are remarkably cheaper for the time being. Heather and I give it two thumbs up!

Tax season has rolled around again. Some people are happy, and some people are either
A) sad
B) mad
C) physically sick
D) all of the above.

Most folks know, if it is multiple choice, the answer is usually "D" if that's an option… (chuckle). This is the time of year, when "money cometh and money goeth" is spelled the same way, I-R-S.

For many years, Emm and I dealt with the latter. We were in the middle-class bracket and owned nothing, but owed everything. There's something very wrong with that equation. Well, I got tired of my Oscar-winning performances every year once I saw how much we had to pay. You know me—crying, not eating, woe is me, and saying, "We're not going to make it"—that sort of stuff. Emm, he never changed,

(I'm singing) "easy like Sunday morning" on the exterior, but he was tired of this as well.

Well, folks, we put a PLAN in place to buy a house. We let go of fear, we got educated, we got disciplined, we worked hard, and we spent much less to carry out the plan. He took classes about mortgages to be an educated buyer, and I was in charge of closing credit cards and keeping us on a strict budget. It took us two years to get everything in order, then we went to the bank and got prequalified. After that, came the real deal with getting a bank to commit to being our lender. Now that was something else! Was the process intense and tedious?

Gimme a Y, Gimme an E, Gimme an S, what does it spell? YES, YES, YES!

I almost thought I was selling my soul. BUT WE DID IT TOGETHER!!! We got our house in 1999. I was going to get a house with an east and west wing, but I couldn't deal with the haters (hahaha). And then you know, family from Left Armpit, Alabama would want to visit and NEVER go home... (I'm a mess, I know).

For real though, we got a small, but quaint abode that housed a daddy, a mommy, and one to two children comfortably. And because I was a big part of the process, I can carry on today at my house, and I haven't missed a beat. I am proud of myself,

99

yes, indeed! Am I passing this knowledge down to our daughter? NO DOUBT! (that song is on my first CD, "Fulfillment... I've Got To Do It" (SHAMELESS PLUG J)

Husbands, commit to teaching and sharing the household affairs with your wife. If you leave this world first, you want to make sure your wife can continue on, without missing a beat.

Wives, learn. Make yourselves available to learn; it is vital! Again, we must be proactive. In some households, the wife handles the affairs, so wives, keep your husbands abreast of the goings-on. Bottom line, you BOTH should be aware of what is going on.

Next time, I'll share with you what happened in 2001 that impacted my life even to this very day. It is so important to listen to that gut feeling, that inner voice. I did, and thank God I did. My life would have been so different now if I didn't listen 12 years ago. Love ya!!!

THE WOWW FACTOR Blog
THURSDAY, APRIL 11, 2013
I GOT UP AND DID SOMETHING ABOUT IT!

It has been an eventful March for my family and I. My youngest sister Tiana, who is 21 years younger than me, got married to her sweetheart, Kareem on March 22.

Can you believe a 21-year difference? I got one better for you, my mother was pregnant with her and my oldest sister, Denise was pregnant with her son at the same time. In other words, the mama and the daughter were prego together. CAN YOU IMAGINE THAT FOOLISHNESS, JUST MESS!!! I'm still traumatized. (HAHAHA)

Anyway, back to the wedding, it was absolutely beautiful. As I sat and listened, watching the ceremony, the words they had to repeat, were words that seemed to come alive as they were spoken. IN SICKNESS AND IN HEALTH, 'TIL DEATH DO US PART. My insides turned a million times. Who knew this would be my story, sooner rather than later? I surely didn't know. My husband was extremely healthy all his life; I mean the epitome of a healthy man. Then came

*sickness in 2006. He was 51 years old at that time...
CANCER?? NO WAY!! NOT MY MAN, NOT THIS
HEALTHY MAN THAT NEVER HAD A HEADACHE
OR A COLD...WHAT???. By the time it was all said
and done, he would have fought three times. During
every battle, we stayed strong, and he fought hard.
Twice he went into remission. I THANK GOD FOR
GRACE!*

*In 2001, a good friend lost her husband, I believe
she was about 40 years old, and he was around the
same age or a few years older. Her loss bothered me
to the point of not being able to shake a feeling of
unrest. I remember telling Emm how I was feeling,
how I couldn't shake it, and that we must make an
appointment to get a better life insurance policy.
I was always the type of wife, if Emm didn't move
fast enough, I'd do it myself or attempt to. Still, if it
was something that I absolutely needed him for...I
would position myself to be the worse nightmare in
his daytime or that bug/fly that wouldn't go away.
So, I commenced to bugging him, annoying him, and
reminding him that we MUST go take out a better
policy.*

*Let me put it this way. I played that tune until he
danced, oh yeah!!! I didn't have to do it for long
because he couldn't stand anything being repeated.
I became a human CD player that is put on repeat*

playing the same song. (hahaha) Oh yeah, buddy, I knew how to go in.

Well, folks, it worked! I remember us going to an Allstate office, taking our daughter with us, and doing what we needed to do. We sat her between us, my darling husband and me, as we handled his business. He even made sure that our daughter Heather was insured. I remember him looking at me and smiling after he said to the agent, "I want a bigger policy on me, if she (talking about me) goes first, Heather and I will be fine but if I go first, I want her to have no worries." I'm paraphrasing, but that was pretty much what he said.

My brothers and sisters, I beseech you, I beg you, and I implore you to get your affairs in order. You and I both know the worse time to try to think clearly is when you're NOT thinking clearly. We had minimal insurance for a lot of years, but God kept tugging at my heart to get a better policy, and thank God we did it while he was WELL!!! IT IS HARD TO GET INSURANCE IF AT ALL WITH A PRE-EXISTING ILLNESS. I am a witness that the Lord does speak to you and wants us to be prepared IN EVERYTHING.

From this day forward, every time I go to a wedding and hear a minister say "in sickness or in health," it will be different. Believe me, dear hearts.

I would marry Emm all over again, even knowing the end from the beginning. Someone stated during his last battle that they'd rather stay single than to have to endure the pain and sacrifice I encountered. I told the person, "When you truly love someone, it's not a burden or a job." I loved my husband throughout the entire journey. I learned so much from him. I learned patience, faith, trust, peace, endurance, gentleness, long-suffering as I watched this amazing man's journey.

Marriage is not a game; it is WORK. God at the head should be the foundation, and HIS WORD your reference. Also, know this; we all will have some valley experiences in this life, whether married or single. Either way, let's choose to GO THROUGH our valley, NOT STAY in the valley. GOD IS OUR HELPER!

I usually have a lot more comic relief when I write these blogs, so forgive me for not making you laugh too much today. You see, when I begin to press the keys on the computer, I free my mind and allow God to direct me in what is to be said at the time. I have had the pleasure of sharing my story and mentioning the importance of LIFE INSURANCE at different venues that I am requested to sing. It breaks my heart to know how many people admit to having no insurance. I pray these blogs will encourage you to arise and do.

I pray it does for you what the tragedy of my friend losing her spouse did for me. I GOT UP AND DID SOMETHING ABOUT IT.

Many of us say we don't have the money to get insurance. I'm here to tell you. I'm not buying into that EXCUSE. We live in a time when the phrase is, "Can I be real?" or "I'm just keeping it real!" WELL, CAN I BE REAL? We have money to do whatever we want to do; I'm not talking about needs BUT wants. You mean to tell me we can't sacrifice one family dinner out per month, nor do we really need another pair of shoes or another dress, or even another iPad?! I'm sure you get my point. The bottom line is, as my grandmother used to say, 'PEOPLE DO WANT THEY WANT TO DO." LIFE INSURANCE IS NOT A WANT. WE NEED LIFE INSURANCE!!!! AND I'M KEEPING IT REAL!!! I hope you're feeling the love, even though I AM BELLOWING AT YOU!!!! (SMILE)

I have a suggestion. When I want to lock myself into an appointment, or a visit with friends, or a dinner engagement, I pull out my calendar and make a verbal agreed upon date. There it's done and no more of the "you know I'm going to..." or "we should get together..." Now your first step is done. Hopefully, you'll follow through and keep the appointment. I'm telling you, you will feel better, if not now later for sure!

I have been charged by the Lord to speak and write my journey on this subject. I do this because I love God's people, and I don't want anyone to be caught unprepared. We will have no one to blame but ourselves.

Oh yes, one more thing. There is one more sister I didn't mention. She is the sister in between me and our youngest sister Tiana. Annette is 10.5 years older than Tiana and 10.5 younger than me!!! NO BOYS, FOUR GIRLS. THE ANGELS IN HEAVEN PROBABLY SOUNDED THE ALARM and sang HANDEL'S MESSIAH when my parents finally said, "IT IS FINISHED" YA THINK…. GEEZZZ!!!

J BE BLESSED!

THE WOWW FACTOR BLOG
TUESDAY, MAY 21, 2013
WE HAD A P L A N!!!

Spring is here, and day time is longer. I really love that about this time of year. Not too happy with my allergies, but whatcha' gonna do? Spring is a sign of birth, growth, hope, life, and oh so many good things. Seeds that have been planted are now showing a hint of manifestation. What you thought might have died during the cold and mostly dark days are now playing "peep a boo" with you, maybe to your surprise. There are so many lessons to be learned when you think of springtime...

I had my daughter in the spring. May 1st was my daughter, Heather's 21st birthday. She mentioned on April 30 that it was her last day of being a "child." I told her, "Girl, please, you were born a woman." Can you imagine? She was 10 lbs. 9oz. and 21 ½ inches long.

Yes, you read it right, let me spell it out. HEATHER WAS TEN POUNDS, NINE OUNCES!!!! And you wonder why I didn't have any more children? The doctor told me the next child would be bigger! WHAT NEXT CHILD??? IN WHO'S BODY?? Folks, there was no C-section involved here. This was O NATURALE!!! Let me type "SUPERWOMAN" right here. (Alicia Keys, you better sing it!) I told Emm this must definitely be his side of the family because we (my side of the family) don't do stuff like this." (laughing)

Heather has always carried herself in such a mature way. I would always tell her, "Old people make old babies." I was 32, and Emm was 36 years old when she was born. This year for her birthday, I took her to a great restaurant on 51st and Broadway called "Capital Grill." Everything about it was great, the food, the ambiance, and the COST! It was worth it though; 21 is a big deal. As we waited for our appetizers, I had her unscramble an envelope of letters that spelled out her birthday present. Folks, she was floored. It spelled METROPOLITAN OPERA! Yes, I got us tickets to see "Dialogue de Carmelites."

If your first love is football, how excited would you be to get tickets to the Super Bowl, or if your thing is basketball and you got tickets to the NBA championship games? Well, she's a classical vocalist! Need I say more?

I pride myself on thinking of memorable gifts for her birthday. I remember when she was 11 years old, and my husband and I picked her up from school in the middle of the day to take her to Disney Land for a week. We broke the news to her at Kennedy Airport—what the surprise was. Her response to all of this came in a whisper. Everything another child might do, such as scream, jump up and down, or any other expressions that would get the attention of others around, Heather did NOT do. She quietly expressed her shock and disbelief, but she was very, very happy. All in all, her reaction was priceless and too funny! We stayed at the Westgate Resorts; we got an excellent rate for a five-day stay at an absolutely beautiful timeshare resort.

So let me tell you about that journey. When you take advantage of a promotional stay at a timeshare, you must schedule an appointment to hear their presentation so that you may perhaps buy a timeshare unit. They are banking on you buying a unit. They will accept nothing less. That's the point of these promotional, well-discounted vacation getaways. Emm and I had a PLAN, though. We would go and listen, but we will stick to our PLAN of not buying a timeshare right now, the bottom line was we were in no position to buy right now. We knew how pushy these reps could be, but we had a PLAN.

Have you noticed how I put the word PLAN in caps? Yes, folks, we had a PLAN. Emm would be the one to take this rep on if they got belligerent because they can. I would just remain quiet and let my man handle this. We knew how this worked because we went on one trip to Pennsylvania when timeshares were first introduced, and I mean it was brutal. The process included much aggressive behavior and rudeness from these reps, and they had the nerve to play the tag team game. Really? Well, THE BARNES tag-team came out in full blast. I was so shocked; I mean, we literally got up out of there. They were too persistent, I mean every time we'd say, "No, thank you,." They'd come back with something.

Ultimately we won; we were both on the same page. In the words of one of the character's on IN LIVIN' COLOR... "DON'T NOBODY MESS WITH MS JENKINS". In other words, DON'T NOBODY MESS WITH THE BARNES AND WIN (hahaha). The way I reenacted everything all the way home would have been torture for most of you, but Emm just chilled and listened to my song and dance, or should I say ranting and raving! After a while, I'm sure he tuned me out, and I didn't care though, as long as he just looked like he was listening, it was all good.

Back to the point of the story, because of this experience, we had already prepared and braced ourselves for the meeting. Don't get me wrong; there is nothing wrong with timeshares; we were just not financially ready for that at that time or when we went to Florida. Our meeting was scheduled a few days after being there. How strategic on their part, let us really enjoy the place first, and then reel us in. That didn't matter though. We knew we'd have a great time there. It came highly recommended, and we were indeed impressed. But, yet and still, we had a PLAN!!!

We went to our appointment early that morning, and we reminded each other to stick to the PLAN. We will tolerate them for this 90-minute presentation and bow out gracefully. We had a wonderful, very polite young man, not aggressive or abrasive at all. He took us around the grounds and showed us different units of possible choices. I must say it was quite impressive, but no matter what, we had a PLAN.

So by the end of all of this, he asked, "So what do you want to do?" Now, remember y'all we had a PLAN. In my head, I said, "Poor, poor guy, you are now going to get this bad news after all the time you spent with us." I felt sorry for him, but that's life!

Well, the time had come. I thought, again, "Baby, go easy on him." Anyone that knew Emm, knew that when it came to business, he was DIRECT, STRAIGHT TO THE POINT, DONE!!! I think all those years at IBM taught him that. Well, Mr. Barnes, my man, my strong-minded man, my man that exudes confidence,

111

my man that I knew would stick to the PLAN, my boo said, "I THINK I WOULD LIKE TO BUY A UNIT."

Okay, folks, this is the conversation I had in my head...

HUH?? SAY WHAT??? I MUST GET THAT WAX BUILD UP OUT OF MY EARS... DID HE JUST SAY I WOULD LIKE TO BUY ONE?? DID YOU FORGET THE PLAN?? YOU KNOW...THE PLAN.... THE PLAN, PLAN!!!! YOU'RE KIDDIN ME, RIGHT??? WHY IS MR REP GRINNING?? OH YEAH THE COMMISSION!!! AWWW LOOK AT HEATHER SHE IS SO EXCITED, SHE THINKS WE WILL BE COMING HERE OR ONE OF THEIR MANY, MANY OTHER RESORTS EVERY YEAR, AWWWW!!!!! I DON'T CARE....EMM THE PLAN, WE HAD A PLAN.......

THE WOWW FACTOR BLOG
THURSDAY, AUGUST 8, 2013

DO THE RIGHT THING!!!!

It's been a long few months, and I've thought of you guys a lot. There is so much I want to share with you, but I really can't tell it all. I will highlight a few things.

First, I am becoming an expert at picking up quickly when someone is trying to take advantage of me, "the emotional widow." So they think! MAN, PLEASE ... I can smell you a mile away...SNIFF, SNIFF, HERE COMES ANOTHER ONE ... (SANGIN') ANOTHER BITES THE DUST!!!!! Don't get me wrong. I am not the angry, emotional, "I-can't-think-I'm-so-confused WIDOW." I just have come up against some DUDES that think I will accept anything where business dealings are concerned, but I'm NOT that one. You've confused me with the one that still doesn't know how to write a check. She's one town over, buddy!

People, surround yourself with people that love you and will help you when you don't know. I have a wonderful father and pastor that are quite influential in my life, two wonderful men that help me so much. NO MAN IS AN ISLAND!

I had something that needed to be fixed in the house, and the person didn't complete the job. I guess he thought he could take advantage and make me wait until Christmas comes, or when Jesus comes, or when HE CHOOSES to come to finish the job. NOPE! WRONG SCENE, WRONG PLAY!!!!

My daughter watched as I handled my business, and still, I came out smelling like roses. Since I could never catch up with him, I gave his son the message to thank him for what he did. I left a check for the half that he did do, and I told his son that I'd get someone else to finish his father's work. That is exactly what I did. By the way, he was in his house the whole time I was talking to his son, but he didn't know I knew he was there. So, when I relayed my message, I turned on my internal microphone so that his whole house could hear me (hahaha). The sad thing is that he just lost some referrals. In the words of Sanford (from Red Foxx's SANFORD AND SON), BIG DUMMY!!!!

Life is so very challenging when you go from being able to support your spouse as head of the household to being head of household. Every step I make, I must consider so much. What makes it all doable is because

I was a part of the process from the beginning of the marriage. I'm not just talking financially but in all areas. Having a plan is a necessity; it might change along the way, but start with something. Learn to budget your money and be disciplined early in life, even before getting married. I give thanks to my mom for teaching me that.

For example, when I shop, I know how to shop, and I know when to quit. I'm always looking down the road... my retirement, Heather's wedding, traveling in ministry, and continuing to pay on my LIFE INSURANCE (I had to put in that plug).

Once again, I have to speak on this LIFE INSURANCE thing. YES, I'M GONNA PLAY THAT TUNE AGAIN. People are still making excuses to me as to why they can't afford it. In my mind, I want to say, "Tell that to your loved ones that you will leave behind. Go ahead and let them know that they will have to go through an embarrassing ordeal of calling Ray-Ray, Ant Bee, Uncle Roscoe, or Pookie and Nem for money. Also, remind your fam to ask their Pastor, 'GOD IS GOOD ALL THE TIME AND ALL THE TIME GOD IS GOOD,' to raise a 'love offering'" on this coming Sunday before you meet with the funeral director. Oh, yes, and remind your loved ones that when they get to the funeral home, they will have to engage in an embarrassing dialogue of 'I'm still getting the money together,' and then your dearest loved ones will be told nothing will be done until they get the money to the funeral home. Oh, yeah, and your grieving loved ones will have to call the rest of the family and tell them the funeral will be in three weeks, maybe."

I know I kind of painted a comical and exaggerated picture, but how do you think they come up with great T.V. shows? FOLKS, IT' IS ART IMITATING LIFE. THIS IS REAL STUFF! (Give me a moment. I'm hysterically laughing as I write this because this has been in somebody's movie or sitcom. So sad.) The bottom line, as my grandmother used to say, "PEOPLE DO WHAT THEY WANT TO DO." FOLKS, WAKE UP, AND DO THE RIGHT THING!!!!

Ok, I have gathered myself. I can be so passionate sometimes. Hey, it's the way I'm made, No apologies. On another note, from the last blog, remember the timeshare saga? Lol. Well, the conclusion to the whole matter is that I still have the timeshare that Heather and I are enjoying. It all worked out. Emm and I sacrificed a lot along the way to keep it, but it was so worth it. I couldn't even really get upset with him. My husband barely bought anything for himself; he called himself a renaissance man. I called him Fred Flintstone (hahaha). I mean, he never used his cell phone, and periodically he lost it. So funny ...

Brothers and sisters, I am still adjusting to going from wife and mother to being a mom only. I loved being both. Someone told me that I am a person before being a wife or a mom. I know and understand that. But I loved being a wife. I enjoyed that role, and I miss it.

BUT STILL, I RISE.

Be blessed!
B. Renee

Scriptures for Your Journey

Here are some scriptures that have helped me through life's journey. May you be encouraged by these scriptures as well.

***

JOSHUA 1:9 (NIV)
9 Have I not commanded you? Be strong and courageous. Do not be afraid; do not be discouraged, for the LORD your God will be with you wherever you go."

***

* * *

2 TIMOTHY 1:7 (KJV)
7 For God hath not given us the spirit of fear;
but of power, and of love, and of a sound
mind.

* * *

PROVERBS 4:20-21 (KJV)
20 My son, attend to my words; incline thine
ear unto my sayings.
21 Let them not depart from thine eyes; keep
them in the midst of thine heart.

* * *

PSALM 56:8 NLT
8 You keep track of all my sorrows. You have
collected all my tears in your bottle. You have
recorded each one in your book.

* * *

PHILIPPIANS 4:6 [NLT]
6 Don't worry about anything; instead, pray
about everything. Tell God what you need,
and thank him for all he has done.

***

MATTHEW 6:31-34 (KJV)

31 Therefore take no thought, saying, What shall we eat? or, What shall we drink? or, Wherewithal shall we be clothed?

32 (For after all these things do the Gentiles seek:) for your heavenly Father knoweth that ye have need of all these things.

33 But seek ye first the kingdom of God, and his righteousness; and all these things shall be added unto you.

34 Take therefore no thought for the morrow: for the morrow shall take thought for the things of itself. Sufficient unto the day is the evil thereof.

***

1 JOHN 5:14-15 (KJV)

14 And this is the confidence that we have in him, that, if we ask any thing according to his will, he heareth us:

15 And if we know that he hear us, whatsoever we ask, we know that we have the petitions that we desired of him.

***

* * *

PSALM 61:2 (KJV)
2 From the end of the earth will I cry unto
thee, when my heart is overwhelmed: lead me
to the rock that is higher than I

* * *

PSALM 38:15 (KJV)
15 For in thee, O LORD, do I hope: thou wilt
hear, O Lord my God

* * *

About the Author

Daughter, sister, auntie, wife, mother, and now a widow. Throughout B. Renée's various stages in life, it was never a thought that becoming a widow was part of the plan. Growing up in church and singing gospel music for the majority of her life was something that was and always would be a significant part of her journey, as well as being the very source that would help keep her grounded.

In 2004, B. Renée Ministries was birthed. Not understanding the weight of what the word "ministries" would evoke, the inevitable would occur. When prophetically spoken that she would bring about her first gospel music cd, God had also begun her transformation from Belinda Renee to now being appointed B. Renée. The Lord spoke to her with these words, "Whenever you write or say, "B. Renee," remember that the "B" will not stand for Belinda, but it will stand for "be." The word "be" means to exist in and abide in who I've called you to be. Remember to B(e) Renée."

After the death of her husband, she began to see and understand the word 'ministries' that was placed at the end of her name. B. Renée had always been a gifted singer, to say the least. God gifted her to write poetry, which had also been something gifted to her mother, who was an astute poet as well. B. Renée, along with her sister Molinda, would write and produce songs on each of her albums, hence, enhancing the development of the author she is today.

Fairly quickly after her husband passed, she began her course with writing blogs and then progressed to creating a widows/widowers group. Ministries . . . now it makes sense. The story doesn't end when you read the last page of this book. There are various streams of B. Renée Ministries yet to blossom. God knows all of what is to come, and B. Renée's answer has been and always will be, "YES LORD, YES!!!"

This predestined path for her life is not one she would have chosen voluntarily and not one that anyone else would have chosen either. It was never a thought in her mind that she would be widowed in her mid 50's. Ultimately, the gifts that God has planted within her have granted her an opportunity to spread the love of Jesus Christ through so many opportunities.

Being a USAF veteran herself, currently, B. Renée is very much dedicated to serving other veterans at one of the many veteran facilities on the east coast. However, her greatest accomplishments were leading her husband to Christ, being a mother, and the best daughter and sister she can possibly be.

For More Information

B. RENÉE MINISTRIES
P.O. BOX 397
NEW YORK, NY 10037

Email: BReneeMinistries@gmail.com
Tele: 646.847.8437
Website: www.TWOVillage.org

To invite B. Renée for an event or conference, to share her story or to introduce The T.W.O. Village support group, or to minister in song, please contact:

Molinda McDaniel
Fellowship Artist Mgmt
Tele: 646.694.8606
Fax: 866.208.8606
Email: FellowshipArtistMgmt@gmail.com